THE BATTLE FOR HELMAND
The Paras in Southern Afghanistan

Dedicated to those who made the ultimate sacrifice

THE BATTLE FOR HELMAND

The Paras in Southern Afghanistan

Collated by Lt Col D J Reynolds QVRM

Acknowledgements.

This book has been collated as a tribute to the men of the UK Task Force who were the first British troops to deploy to Southern Afghanistan in 2006. It has been published by DRA Publishing and Pegasus, the journal of The Parachute Regiment and Airborne Forces, as a record of regimental history. It would not have been possible without the support of Brigadier Ed Butler, Lt Col Stuart Tootal, the company commanders who supplied their Pegasus Notes as well as the many contributions from the supporting units of 16 Air Assault Brigade.

The high quality pictorial content of this publication is due to the many photographers who supported the project. Cpl Rob Knight and Cpl Mike Fletcher of the RLC who deployed to Helmand as Army photographers and captured some amazing images, which are Crown Copyright. Recognition must also go to Sean Langan, the television documentary maker who was in Garmser at the height of the fighting and covered the entire deployment. Andrew Chittock who visited the Task Force in August and September, and Dilip Banerjee of DPL; Yves DeBay who has covered almost every war in the past 20 years; Patrick Allen the specialist aviation photographer, who took many of the Chinook images; Karl Voosam who took the images of an Army Lynx inside Musa Qaleh. Thanks must also go to Pulitzer prize winner James Hill, whose father served with the Regiment, and has allowed us to use his award winning images of the Taliban. International photographer Ed Grazda also supported the book as did the internationally acclaimed photographer Gary Trotter. Kind thanks must also go to Jason Sutcliffe of the Sunday Times and Andy Bush of the Sun who allowed their photographs to be used. Sapper Magazine kindly supported the project as did the Ministry of Defence.

Front page: The General Purpose Machine Gun, a familiar sight to all who served at Sangin, draped with the Victoria Cross medal won by Cpl Bryan Budd of A Company 3 PARA.

DRA Publishing, 14 Mary Seacole Road, The Millfields, Plymouth PL1 3JY.

Designed by Ez Creative

//CONTENTS

Brigadier Ed Butler CBE DSO

//COMMANDER UK TASK FORCE
//FOREWORD

My six months as Commander British Forces Afghanistan, in 2006, was the most challenging and risk intensive command tour I have undertaken in my career. Over the six bloody and ferocious months in Helmand Province the 3 PARA Battle Group was involved in some 500 contacts, with half a million rounds of small arms and over 13,000 artillery and mortar rounds being fired. It saw the blooding of the Apache attack helicopter and the Joint Helicopter Force flying over 100 CASEVAC (Casualty Evacuation, often by helicopter) missions to extract some 170 casualties – with sadly 33 KIA (Killed in Action). Contacts could last for six – eight hours, with paratroopers fighting in 50 degrees centigrade and carrying 70lb of equipment 'fighting order'. Young men quickly matured beyond their years, battle hardened by an intensity not witnessed since the Korean War. Some would spend weeks fighting and sleeping in their body armour and helmets, often snatching no more than a few minutes rest between enemy attacks, and drinking water the temperature of a decent brew. Phenomenal stuff.

Hundreds of Taliban were killed and injured, but not once was I in any doubt that the Battle Group was in danger of being defeated. By the end of the summer the Taliban had been tactically beaten, deciding to take on the members of 16 Air Assault Brigade in a conventional and attritional fight. In my judgement the Taliban seriously underestimated the professionalism, raw courage and self-belief of the Airborne soldier; the current wearers of the maroon beret more than live up to the reputation of their forefathers.

The cost of this 'break-in' battle into southern Afghanistan was high in blood and treasure and we will never forget those brave men who paid the ultimate sacrifice, including Cpl Bryan Budd VC and Cpl Mark Wright GC, daring all to win all. All their names, along with the towns of Now Zad, Musa Qaleh, Sangin and Gereshk will remain firmly listed in regimental history. And rightly so.

People often ask me what Afghanistan is all about and whether it is worth it. To me delivering success in that country is essential for a variety of strategic reasons. The Brigade deployed in April 2006 to make a difference to the ordinary Afghan. Not only did the brave men and women of the force make a genuine difference, but they also set some really solid foundations for the Other Government Departments, the Royal Marines and subsequent follow on forces to build upon. Although there is still plenty to do in Afghanistan across all lines of operation, the Airborne community, serving and retired, can be hugely proud of the Brigade's achievements. I for one am.

I salute the courage and endeavours of all those who I was privileged to lead across the UK Task Force, 16 Air Assault Brigade and especially those in the 3 PARA Battle Group.

Brigadier Ed Butler CBE DSO
Commander UK Task Force
Helmand

//COMMANDING OFFICER 3 PARA
//PREFACE

The deployment of 3 PARA BG to Helmand in 2006, was primarily to deliver a safe and secure environment in support of the Government of Afghanistan in order to allow reconstruction to take place. Instead the Battle Group faced a brutal 'break in battle' and experienced some of the most intense war-fighting for a generation. Our soldiers rose to the challenge and in every engagement the enemy were convincingly overmatched. By the end of the tour it was clear that we had inflicted a tactical defeat on the enemy and created the conditions for the next formation and follow-on battle groups and development agencies to build on. However, the cost in blood and treasure was, not insignificant and this book salutes the men and women who served with the Battle Group and UKTF and particularly pays special respect to those who made the ultimate sacrifice.

Lieutenant Colonel S J C Tootal DSO OBE
Commanding Officer 3 PARA Battle Group

The Taliban emerged in the mid 1990s. After their defeat in the north and Kabul in 2001 their last major battle was at Kandahar. Those who survived fled south to Helmand and the neighbouring provinces.

Fields of poppies colour the Helmand landscape prior to harvest time. The opium that the fields of southern Afghanistan deliver is controlled by the Taliban who monitor production across the Province and manage its exportation.

10

→ **INTRODUCTION**

The Taliban, well armed and committed, attempted to undermine the Government of Afghanistan in 2006 and fragment Hamid Karzai's (pictured below) plans to expand security and reconstruction to the south of the country.

//THE PLAYERS

Hamid Karzai was elected President of the Islamic Republic of Afghanistan in 2004, having received 55% of the national vote. Karzai and Abdul Haq were the two Pashtun leaders who rose to prominence after 9/11. Karzai entered Afghanistan from Quetta just prior to the US invasion and was able to persuade local tribes to end their support for the Taliban while Abdul Haq approached from Peshawar on a similar mission. Both were key in support of Coalition operations against the Taliban during this period and while Karzai evaded capture by the Taliban, Haq was not so fortunate and was summarily executed. In Helmand, Karzai's representative was Mohammad Daoud, who was appointed Governor of the Province in early 2006. The Provincial Governor is the main representative of the central government in Helmand.

The Taliban in Helmand were alleged to be more than 2,000 strong in early 2006. This figure was not official, but it was widely reported in the media. However, there was no factual evidence to substantiate these claims, instead the evidence indicated that the Taliban were no bigger in number than 200, and their presence had been identified by Coalition partners. While there was concern that the Taliban was preparing to increase their force in southern Afghanistan, this was all speculation. Across Helmand, the Taliban and their criminal warlords who ran the region were directed by Mullah Dadullah, who carried a reputation for extreme brutality. He had joined forces with the Taliban at its formation in 1994 and was known simply as the Black Mullah, a term generated as a result of his ruthless violence and use of torture. He reported to Mullah Omar, the one eyed leader of the Taliban across the entire country, who was believed to be hiding in the tribal areas of the border. At the top of the terrorist tree and always hiding from the Coalition was Osama Bin Laden, who was behind the 9/11 attacks on the USA.

//INTRODUCTION
//AFGHANISTAN

After decades of fighting the Soviets, Afghanistan had within a few years of the Russian departure in 1988 become a lawless state. Warlords across the country fought to retain their spoils and resulted in Mujihadeen factions seizing power. However, ethnic fighting broke out between the Pashtun, Tajiks, Uzbeks, Hazaras and Turkmen. In October 1994, the Taliban, otherwise known at the time as the Islamic students movement, under Mullah Omar, emerged to challenge the Mujihadeen government. The Taliban promised to restore peace and security and pledged to enforce strict Sharia, or Islamic law. They seized Kandahar and attempted to eliminate the Mujihadeen. In September 1995, the Taliban took the western province of Herat, which borders Iran, followed by the seizure of bases belonging to the Pashtun leader Hekmatyar in the south. The push continued until September 1996, when the Taliban took Kabul. Sharia law was instituted in Kabul in October of that year. Girls schools were closed, women were banned from working and forced to stay indoors unless accompanied by a close relative; music, television and sport, were outlawed. A year later, in May 1997, the Taliban forces took Faryab province in the northwest, and the eastern city of Mazar-i-Sharif. In July, the anti-Taliban Northern Alliance took Parwan province. At this time, the UN began peace talks; however, these collapsed in May 1998 and Taliban forces launched a northern offensive. Calls for a cease-fire by the United Nations (UN) were ignored, and there were reports from human rights groups that several thousand ethnic Hazaras had been massacred. Following the bombing on US embassies in Dar es Salaam and Nairobi by Al Qaeda, the USA launched cruise missiles at targets inside Afghanistan stating that they were attacking terrorist training camps.

US and UN workers were pulled out of Afghanistan and it was not until March 1999 that UN staff returned. Peace talks failed as fresh fighting broke out between the Taliban and warlords. The US imposed trade sanctions on the Taliban in July 1999, threatening military action and the Taliban summer offensive in the North was a failure, though some 140,000 people were made homeless as a result of the fighting. The grip of the government on the areas north of Kabul did improve. Then in November 1999, the UN imposed an air embargo on the Taliban. In January 2000, the Taliban government recognized the rebel Islamic Chechen government, aggravating the Russians. Training camps across Afghanistan were now being used to train Al Qaeda fighters who had arrived from the Middle East to pledge their suicidal commitment to Osama Bin Laden's plan to attack the USA in 2001.

The graveyard of crippled Soviet armour litters the country and acts as a constant reminder of the years of the Russian occupation.

Following terrorist attacks on New York and Washington on 11th September 2001, UK forces joined Coalition operations in what has become known as the War on Terror. In October 2001, Royal Navy nuclear submarines fired Tomahawk missiles against Taliban and Al Qaeda networks; while RAF aircraft provided reconnaissance and air-to-air refueling capabilities in support of US strike aircraft. UK troops were first deployed in November 2001, when specialist units from 16 Air Assault Brigade deployed to secure Bagram airfield alongside Royal Marines. On 13th November, the Northern Alliance, supported by Coalition forces, took Kabul and the Taliban fled south to their spiritual home at Kandahar where they were surrounded by US forces at the airport and forced to surrender on 7th December 2001. In January 2002, the 2nd Battalion The Parachute Regiment deployed to the Capital as part of NATO's international peace keeping force, called ISAF (International Security Assistance Force). ISAF's primary role was, and remains, to support the Government of Afghanistan (GOA) in providing and maintaining a secure environment in order to facilitate the re-building of Afghanistan. The ISAF presence in Afghanistan includes many of the NATO nations who have personnel deployed across the country.

Taliban forces in Helmand province remained strong in 2001 and while the outside world celebrated the surrender of the Taliban in Kandahar, others remained in control of Helmand. Those Taliban who could escape from Kandahar airfield fled to Helmand, among them the Taliban leader, Mullah Omar. During their campaign in Afghanistan the Soviets had deployed into Helmand and laid significant minefields in an attempt to restrict the movement of the Mujihadeen.

Following the defeat of the Taliban in 2001, US forces mounted operations in southern Afghanistan, but these deployments were small and mainly focussed on small-scale hearts and minds operations by US Special Forces. The Taliban therefore remained potent in Helmand with total control of the poppy harvest and local people. Before the Soviet invasion, Helmand was a wealthy agricultural area. But irrigation systems had collapsed in the years of the Jihad waged against the Soviets, and opium poppies became the only viable crop.

Afghanistan held its first democratic elections in 2004 and in September of the same year the UK deployed six Harrier GR7s to Kandahar to support Coalition operations. In February 2005, NATO announced that ISAF would expand its security presence into the West of Afghanistan. This process began on 31st May 2005, when ISAF took command of two Italian-led Provincial Reconstruction Teams (PRTs) in the provinces of Herat and Farah and of a Forward Support Base in Herat, also provided by Italy. Later that year two further ISAF-led PRTs in the West became operational, in Chagcharan, led by Lithuania, and Qaleh-ye-Now, led by Spain. The staged NATO expansion, under ISAF, had a positive role in extending the writ of the Kabul government to the provinces, setting the conditions for reconstruction, and in helping the Afghan authorities provide security during the successful presidential elections in October 2004.

There was to be little time for Peace Support Operations. Instead the Paras experienced in the words of Lt General David Richards, top right, who commanded all NATO forces in Afghanistan during 2006, some of the most intense fighting since Korea.

These elections were a crucial milestone in the democratic development of the country, and the parliamentary elections in September 2005 marked the successful culmination of the Bonn Process. (The Bonn Agreement took place in 2001)

The London Conference on Afghanistan in January 2006, successfully created the framework for the next phase of development in Afghanistan. At the same time the then UK Defence Secretary John Reid announced the deployment of 3,300 British military personnel, centred initially around 16 Air Assault Brigade, to Helmand. The force was to be robust and the final package would include armoured reconnaissance vehicles and artillery as well as Apache Attack helicopters and troop carrying Chinooks. It would also include contingents from Denmark and Estonia. In March and April the lead elements of the 3rd Battalion The Parachute Regiment Battle Group arrived in Helmand with attached forces from Denmark and Estonian. Royal Engineers, with force protection from the Royal Marines, had built a huge camp in the middle of the desert in preparation of the UK Task Force's arrival. In May 2006 the UK deployed the HQ of the Allied Rapid Reaction Corps (ARRC) to Kabul for nine months to lead the ISAF, and oversee expansion of NATO security into the more challenging south and east of Afghanistan.

The main effort for the Task Force was to focus on providing security and stability in order to allow the delivery of reconstruction. But, the Taliban had already issued a 'warning order' to British forces via the international media. However, the aim for UK Plc remained on Peace Support Operations.

But within weeks of British troops arriving the UK media reported that the 3 PARA Battle Group had been engaged in heavy firefights with Taliban insurgents. A senior British officer in Kabul, the base of the NATO headquarters, reported that more than 100 soldiers from 16 Air Assault Brigade had supported Afghan troops and police in fighting off attacks by hundreds of Taliban fighters. There was to be little time for Peace Support Operations. Instead 3 PARA Battle Group faced a 'break-in battle' into Helmand in which they were to experience in the words of General David Richards, the British commander of NATO forces in Kabul, 'some of the most intense warfighting seen since Korea.'

The Taliban appeared to recruit their fighters from the tribal villages between Pakistan and Afghanistan. Their aim was to restore Sharia law across Afghanistan, which prevented girls from being educated and even banned the national sport of kite flying.

//INTRODUCTION
//THE TALIBAN AND AL QAEDA

The Taliban's total intolerance of the non-Muslim world was symbolised by the demolition of the giant and ancient Buddhas carved out of cliffs at Bamiyan in 2001. Fighting broke out after the Soviets left as warlords fought for regional control. Warlords in the north of the country formed the Northern Alliance and fought the Taliban for control of their land. The prevailing chaos and huge number of refugees made the country the ideal base for Osama Bin Laden's Al Qaeda network. The former Saudi businessman gathered his exiled followers in Afghanistan as well as other militants from Yemen, the Sudan, and other countries. This new force of Taliban fighters rejected all aspects of conservative and peaceful Muslim rule.

In 1998, Bin Laden's cohorts were accused of being behind the bombing of US embassies in Nairobi, which killed 247 and at Dar-es-Salem where ten died. In response the US Navy was directed to attack Afghanistan and Sudan. Cruise missiles were launched at suspected Al Qaeda training camps inside Afghanistan and at what was believed to be an Al Qaeda chemical plant in Sudan. After the 9/11 attacks on the US, Coalition forces deployed to Afghanistan and linked up with the Northern Alliance to launch an offensive to depose the Taliban. Within weeks both the Taliban and Al Qaeda were on the run and quickly defeated. But many Taliban fighters fled south, heading for Helmand.

//INTRODUCTION
//HELMAND

Helmand is one of 34 provinces that make up Afghanistan with a population of more than one million. The Helmand river flows through the mainly desert region and the capital Lashkar Gah, which was the centre of a US development programme in the 1960s. The project laid out tree-lined streets in Lashkar Gah, built a network of irrigation canals and constructed a large hydroelectric dam resulting in the area being dubbed 'little America'. But the USAID program was abandoned when the communists seized power in 1978. Nearly three decades later, the unforgiving heat of Helmand, its arid terrain and unmarked minefields provided a significant challenge to the 3 PARA Battle Group. Helicopters and air transport were key to the formation's manoeuvrability, while the fitness of individual soldiers, who often carried ammunition and water weighing in excess of 80lbs was paramount. The Soviet occupation and the subsequent ethnic fighting, was followed by a period of extreme hardship under the Taliban, which left Afghanistan impoverished and facing an extended humanitarian problem. Infrastructure outside Kabul had collapsed which consequently hindered the government's ability to deliver basic health, education and social services. In many remote areas of the country, such as Helmand, children had little or no access to education or basic public services and the Taliban had moved to fill this vacuum, they saw themselves as the new warlords of the decade with the opium trade being at the core of their business. Helmand sits in the opium-producing region called the 'Golden Crescent' and produces at least one third of the world's heroin each year. Taliban gangs pay local farmers a pittance for their crops, which are then smuggled out of the country in what is a drugs trade worth allegedly US $1.5 million. These profits clearly provide the potential to generate revenue to support Taliban operations. Afghans are typically friendly and hospitable, but their lives have been rife with conflict and they can be stern. Perceptions are generally influenced by faith that Allah controls everything and that everything happens according to his will. This belief helps Afghans tolerate extreme hardships. Islamic law forbids the consumption of alcohol and pork, and most people comply. Many men smoke local tobacco, hashish and opium. The cultural honour of Afghans is complex, it plays a major role in rural life and upholding family pride is paramount. For British troops deploying to Helmand cultural education was part of their pre-deployment package and lessons in which soldiers learned to only eat with their right hand proved important to those who attended Shuras (meeting with local Afghan elders). Helmand is a desolate drought ridden region, with limited roads.

Prior to the arrival of British troops it was also one of the most lawless areas in the world, with the Taliban constantly trying to undermine the Afghan government and its representatives in the south. In early 2006 the Taliban had announced, via the media, that the British Army would be defeated if it deployed to southern Afghanistan and claimed they had hundreds of fighters armed and ready, but it was unclear where they were being recruited. The Taliban were well armed, adaptable and cunning. They knew the areas of southern Afghanistan well and had proven success on the battlefield. Tactically they appeared to well organised with procedures to evacuate injured fighters and the ability to re-supply their front line. In the weeks leading up to the arrival of the 3 PARA Battle Group, the Taliban launched a propaganda campaign to try and undermine the good intent of the UK Task Force. They, wrongly, claimed that history had recorded that British troops had always been defeated in Afghanistan. But, in the words of one British Army officer, 'they (the Taliban) had not faced The Parachute Regiment before'.

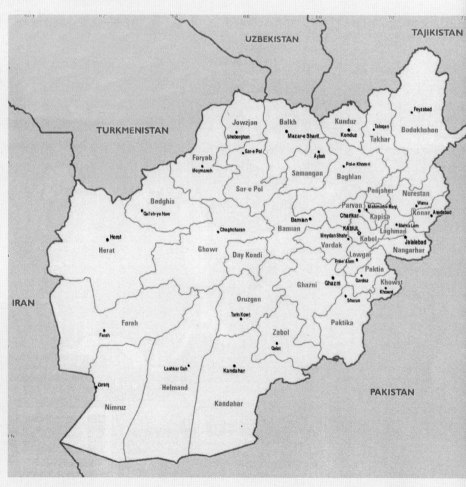

17

The 3 PARA Battle Group spent almost ten months preparing for their deployment to Helmand.

The training, particularly the fitness, paid dividends for the Battle Group once in Afghanistan.

//INTRODUCTION
//TRAINING FOR WAR

In November 2005, the Minister for the Armed Forces, Adam Ingram, announced that British preparations for a possible deployment to Afghanistan in 2006 were to begin and he added that 16 Air Assault Brigade would commence contingency training in preparation for any deployment. In his speech to the House of Commons on 14th November 2005, he said: "As previously announced by the Prime Minister, the United Kingdom is committed to deploy the Headquarters Group of the Allied Rapid Reaction Corps to lead the International Security Assistance Force (ISAF) from May 2006 to February 2007. In addition, the Secretary of State for Defence has previously informed the House (7th July 2005) of preliminary plans to support the expansion of ISAF by establishing a British-led Provincial Reconstruction Team in the province of Helmand, in Southern Afghanistan. The aim of both would be to help restore Afghanistan as a secure and stable state, and prevent the country again becoming a haven for global terrorists. The ISAF is led by NATO, which is currently planning the expansion of the ISAF into the south and east of Afghanistan. Once these plans mature, individual Allies, including the United Kingdom, will be able to take final decisions on deployment. In advance of this, however, it is sensible to begin British preparations for a potential deployment. These are necessarily based upon national planning assumptions which may need to be adapted in the light of NATO's conclusions and the final positions taken by individual Allies and Partners, including the UK. In the first instance, the tempo of work to prepare the ground in Helmand for a possible British deployment is being increased. These activities are initially likely to involve some 250 troops. Preparations are also underway in the United Kingdom. Some units, predominantly drawn from 16 Air Assault Brigade and the Joint Helicopter Command, will shortly commence collective training on a contingency basis. Similarly, the procurement of certain equipment enhancements that may be needed for a deployment of this nature is underway. These necessary measures are prudent military preparations for a possible future deployment. They do not mean that these units or capabilities will be committed to Southern Afghanistan in 2006. No final decisions have yet been made. Should the United Kingdom decide to commit additional forces to the ISAF in 2006, a full statement will then be made to the House as soon as possible."

Back in August 2005, the 3rd Battalion The Parachute Regiment had been warned off for potential operations in Helmand. While the official announcement had still not been released there was much media speculation that 16 Brigade would head the UK force destined for southern Afghanistan in 2006. 3 PARA and all leading elements of 16 Air Assault Brigade undertook a wide range of specialist training packages to hone their core skills, which were then validated in a major exercise at Otterburn. This included an air assault phase, live firing, night attacks, heli-insertions and advance to contact drills.

The training was intense and pushed the Battle Group to its limitations in order to make sure that every aspect of war fighting was revised, just in case the Taliban came out to take on the UK force. As units waited for the official government announcement, 3 PARA and the Battle Group focussed on physical fitness in order to prepare for the intense heat and arid conditions that would face them in the spring and summer of 2006. New equipment was issued and the Operational Pre-deployment and Training package attended. In January 2006, 16 Air Assault Brigade and the 3 PARA BG took part in their final pre-deployment training alongside Estonian and Danish troops who would be attached to the Battle Group in Helmand. Exercise HERRICK EAGLE took place at Copehill training village on Salisbury Plain, at the same time as the official announcement of the UK force was announced. Standing guard beside a Land Rover laden with Milan anti-tank missiles, Private Peter Evans of 3 PARA said he was "keeping an open mind" about what he would find in Afghanistan, but was in little doubt that his training would see him through the challenges. The exercise included a parachute drop in order to prepare the battalion should it be required to mount an airborne assault in Helmand. This was the sixth jump within 12 months for B Company and noteably one of the more airborne members of the company Sgt Kurgan, dropped in chest rig to keep within the weight restrictions. After HERRICK EAGLE the battalion quickly re-grouped and departed for a final exercise where they underwent more rigorous training on Exercise DESERT EAGLE to prepare for every eventuality in Helmand. Based at a remote camp in a middle east country, where the environment replicated southern Afghanistan. Everyone from 3 PARA, the Apache pilots and the key units of 16 Brigade later spoke of the value of the training.

Gunners from 21 Battery on patrol in Lashkar Gah.

The Pathfinders pictured on the ground with US forces during Preliminary operations.

CHAPTERONE
→ **PRELIMINARY OPERATIONS**

The RAF Support Helicopter Force was a key part of Preliminary Operations.

Initial patrols on the ground in Lashkar Gah by members of 21 Battery.

The initial Task Force as announced by the MoD comprised elements of the Headquarters of 16 Air Assault Brigade and an airborne infantry battlegroup, based around 3 PARA. The force was to be supported by eight Apache Attack Helicopters, provided by 9 Regiment, Army Air Corps, on their first operation, and four Lynx Light Utility Helicopters . The RAF was tasked to provide a detachment of six Chinook helicopters. Other major units and capabilities included Scimitar and Spartan armoured vehicles from the Household Cavalry Regiment, a battery of 105mm Light Guns from 7th Parachute Regiment, RHA, an air defence battery to take on the PRT role in Lashkar Gah, a battery of Desert Hawk Unmanned Aerial Vehicles from 32 Regiment, RA (deployed for the first time), 13 Air Assault Regiment, elements of 29 Regiment RLC, 7 Battalion REME and 16 Close Support Medical Regiment.

//PRELIMINARY OPERATIONS
//FIRST ON THE GROUND

In a statement to the House of Commons on 26th January 2006, the then UK defence secretary, Mr John Reid said that the dangers of UK military action in Afghanistan paled in comparison to the risks Britain would face if the international community allowed the country to become a sanctuary for international terrorism again. Abandoning Afghanistan was simply not an option.

Mr Reid said: "Whatever the difficulties and risks of this deployment – and I do not hide them from the house or the country – those risks are nothing compared to the dangers to our country and our people of allowing Afghanistan to fall back into the hands of the Taliban and the terrorists. We will not allow that. And the Afghan people will not allow that."

On the same day the Ministry of Defence made it clear that preliminary operations were about to start. It was announced that an advance party of 850 personnel drawn from 39 Regiment, Royal Engineers and a guard force from 42 Commando Royal Marines would deploy to build a camp in Helmand. In addition troops from the 1st Battalion The Royal Gloucestershire, Berkshire and Wiltshire Regiment were to deploy to Lashkar Gah and Helmand during the preliminary operations phase. Two soldiers died during this period: Corporal Mark Cridge of 7 Signals Regiment and LCpl Peter Edward Craddock of 1st Battalion The Royal Gloucestershire, Berkshire and Wiltshire Regiment. Both were non-combat deaths.

Preliminary operations under the direction of a team from the Joint Task Force Headquarters established a presence in Lashkar Gah and co-ordinated the building of the base in Helmand, to be called Camp Bastion. Situated more than 400 miles south of Kabul in the middle of nowhere the camp was quickly dubbed the 'Alamo' by those building it. The harsh environment presented a challenge to the engineers with temperatures sinking to minus 20°C in the early part of the year and soaring to 50°C by May. Building Camp Bastion from which helicopters and fixed wing transport aircraft could operate was an extraordinary logistical operation unparalleled in modern British military history. The Royal Engineers from 39 Regiment were given only four months to create what was virtually a small town from nothing. Almost everything was flown in by Chinook helicopter and despite the odds the camp was completed on time.

The plan for Helmand was to base the UK brigade headquarters at Kandahar, where it was co-located with the command element of what was called Regional Command South, a Canadian - manned headquarters. This location gave the UK commander, Brigadier Ed Butler, who was also Commander British Forces (COMBRITFOR), the flexibility to liaise regularly with RS-South, shuttle north to Kabul for meetings with General Richards, as well as fly west to Helmand.

At Lashkar Gah, the capital of Helmand the Provincial Reconstruction Team (PRT) was based and further south deep in the desert, the newly constructed Camp Bastion was home to the 3 PARA Battle Group. Close to Bastion was Camp Tombstone, where troops from 7 Para RHA trained the Afghan National Army (ANA) delivering instruction from specialist British Army teams known as the Operational Mentor and Liaison Teams (OMLTs). These soldiers had the task of preparing ANA recruits for front line operations against the Taliban.

The deployment into Afghanistan saw A Company on the ground first, in early April. The arrival of the 3 PARA Battle Group was complete in southern Afghanistan by 11th May. For the leading elements of the battalion Camp Bastion was a big culture shock. In early April, the camp was austere, with running water only a couple of hours per day, constant power cuts and catering based on field rations. Bastion quickly quadrupled in size, with roads, sewers, and new tents springing up every day. Often on early morning runs, the soldiers found that Engineers had dug a foot deep trench across their normal routes. But the main problem was the dust. It had the consistency of cement mix and when the wind increased, it got everywhere. By early May, Bastion was home to nearly 2000 troops from 3 PARA, 51 Para Sqn RE, 7 Para RHA, 16 CS Regt, 9 Regt AAC, an Estonian Platoon, a Danish Recce Sqn and a host of other key troops. The first paratrooper on the ground was Major Stuart Russell (pictured below in a poppy field), who arrived more than a month ahead of the Battle Group.

23

Camp Bastion starts to take shape as tents are erected. The project was one of the biggest undertaken by the Royal Engineers.

The camp was built from scratch, with Royal Engineers working around the clock to complete the project.

/PRELIMINARY OPERATIONS
//BUILDING CAMP BASTION

In February 2006 an advanced party deployed to Helmand to build a camp for 16 Air Assault Brigade. The unit, 39 Regiment, Royal Engineers, deployed to Helmand province to build the desert base that would become Camp Bastion. The base in the middle of Helmand was a major engineering and logistical challenge. It was to become a small town with its own resources from power to drainage. Bastion, named after the Hesco Bastion protective wall units, was to become home to more than 3,000 troops. In addition it would have its own airstrip for C-130s and a helicopter area for Chinook, Apache and Lynx aircraft.

Pathfinders are picked up by a Chinook during Preliminary operations in Helmand.

The damage to a Pathfinder Land Rover after it hit a mine.

//PRELIMINARY OPERATIONS
//ADVANCE FORCE OPERATIONS

The Pathfinder Group arrived in Afghanistan mid-March 2006, ahead of the main body, and started conducting in theatre training at Kandahar. The main task for the Pathfinders was to act as the 'eyes and ears' of the Task Force identifying threats and collating intelligence. For the deployment, it had been boosted by specialists from across the Battle Group from engineers to medics and was to be known as the Pathfinder Group. After final preparations at Kandahar the Group deployed by C-130 Hercules to a Tactical Landing Zone close to the Helmand Provincial capital of Lashkar Gah. From there it conducted a road move to Forward Operating Base (FOB) PRICE, just outside the strategically important town of Gereshk. Initial operations focussed on reconnaissance around Sangin and Gereshk, in order to build a realistic ground picture for 3 PARA Battle Group.

Once the Area of Operation (AO) at Gereshk had been handed over to the lead elements of 3 PARA the Pathfinder Group headed north, with the aim of collating information about the region for the remainder of the task force. One of these patrols in the vicinity of Now Zad was engaged in a firefight with elements of the Afghan Police, who claimed that they thought the Pathfinders were Taliban; this is a moot point as evidence now suggests that they had been infiltrated by the Taliban.

The next patrol was not without incident. While patrolling to the north-west of Sangin a vehicle hit a mine and one member of the Engineer Recce lost his leg. The Pathfinders then deployed to Lashkar Gah to conduct patrols, primarily aimed at ensuring that the Provincial Reconstruction Team, 21 Battery Royal Artillery, had additional protection for its initial tasks.

Once the Group had returned from Lashkar Gah planning and preparation followed for a patrol once again to the north. The task was to recce Tactical Landing Zones (TLZ) and Helicopter Landing Sites (HLS) and Drop Zones (DZ) for potential parachute operations. No plan survives contact and the patrol was soon extended and headed north onto the Baghram Valley. This was a hazardous journey and the enemy attempted to ambush the Pathfinders on a number of occasions. The patrol ended up in the important town of Musa Qaleh, where its job was to bolster the Afghan Police and show the people a viable alternative to the Taliban. After five days the Pathfinder Group were relieved by a company from the US Army's 2/87th Infantry Regiment. But, later, the Pathfinders would return for a longer stay.

A pause during the action at Musa Qaleh where the Pathfinders were to return later in the tour.

27

Paratroopers arrived in Helmand after months of training, ready for anything.

CHAPTERTWO
→ PREPARING FOR OPERATIONS

The relationship with local people was strong.

British troops made sure they respected local culture and traditions.

//PREPARING FOR OPERATIONS
//THE PLAN FOR HEARTS & MINDS

The UK Task Force and the 3 PARA Battle Group came to Afghanistan to help the Afghan Government to create a secure environment in which development and improved governance could be brought to the Afghan people. The force did not come looking for a fight, but had trained hard to respond robustly if attacked. Their primary aim was to support the Government of Afghanistan by enhancing security and supporting Afghan forces to establish stability in the south of the country. The stability would then allow reconstruction and development work to proceed. The three main objectives included training the Afghan army, providing security for the PRT in Lashkar Gah and delivering security with the main manoeuvre force based at Camp Bastion. The plan to establish and deliver a Hearts and Minds campaign in which the local community could understand why the UK Task Force deployed to Helmand, and that it had come to help at the invitation of the Afghan government was always going to be a challenge. The diverse regional cultures demanded respect and as the first British troops on the ground quickly established a rapport with local people, the Taliban prepared to lure the UK Task Force into battle. They had exercised fear and intimidation for many years in order to maintain control of the poppy harvest which as previously mentioned, funded the insurgents' military campaign and propagated extreme Islamic belief. At the start of 2006, it was estimated that 200 Taliban were seeking to control Helmand and while their grip was strong, some political observers believed security and stability could be quickly achieved by NATO. Prior to the arrival of UK troops, the Taliban had already started their propaganda machine claiming that British forces would be run out of Helmand and warned Afghans not to speak to the Coalition. Despite this, the early weeks of the operation looked promising when efforts to mix with the local community, alongside Afghan forces, and reassure residents, worked well. Local people were friendly and welcoming to UK troops in Lashkar Gah and there appeared to be a local willingness to engage. But this was short lived as the Taliban moved to threaten the community and attack UK forces. Hundreds of young Taliban fighters appeared, some reports claiming more than 2,000. An intense period of fighting commenced in towns which were to become familiar hotspots; Sangin, Musa Qaleh, Gereshk and Now Zad. But the Taliban were not prepared for the professional resolve of British forces and in the first few months hundreds of them were killed. Time after time the soldiers of 3 PARA Battle Group defeated the enemy. Well supported by the aircraft of the RAF and NATO, the effect the soldiers of 3 PARA Battle Group had on the Taliban was significant. This was evident in the fact that the mass attacks by the Taliban against the Government District Centres, where paratroopers were to deploy in support of the Government of Afghanistan, stopped in September 2006 due to the large number of fighters killed. Instead the Taliban focussed on sniper operations, roadside bombs and attempted to get suicide bombers into Lashkar Gah. The UK Task Force had arrived ready to mount a hearts and minds campaign, but instead was forced into a kinetic fight which it took to the Taliban and won. The fighting was raw and bloody and paratroopers were to fight so close to the enemy that they could often see the whites of their eyes. By the time the tour ended in October 2006, the first signs of reconstruction were under way, the Afghan National Army had planned and led its first operation in southern Afghanistan and a peace plan had been agreed in Musa Qaleh, where some of the worst fighting had taken place.

Local people in Helmand lived in fear of the Taliban.

The RAF's C-130 Hercules ferried troops and equipment into Helmand.

Paratroopers arrived at Kandahar and were then flown forward to Bastion to commence operations.

//PREPARING FOR OPERATIONS
//ARRIVAL OF THE TASK FORCE

The main elements of the Battle Group arrived in southern Afghanistan in early May to join the advance party and move into locations at Kandahar, Lashkar Gah and Camp Bastion. A Company, 3 PARA, were the first on the ground and by the second week of May the entire Battle Group was in place and ready for operations. The force included the first operational deployment of the Apache Attack Helicopter and the first Royal Artillery battery to be deployed on operations with the Desert Hawk, Unmanned Aerial Vehicle. As the force prepared for work medical staff established what was a highly impressive hospital and surgical unit, while the Household Cavalry bolted on the special bar armour to their Scimitars and command vehicles to prevent rocket propelled grenades penetrating their vehicles. Located nearby to Bastion, Camp Tombstone was the home of what was called the OMLT (Operational Mentor and Liaison Teams) where 7 Para RHA co-ordinated the required training and mentoring of the Afghan National Army in their final phase of instruction, to ensure they were ready for high intensity operations. Logistics teams and repair crews established themselves at Bastion along with Royal Engineers, including bomb disposal teams known as Explosive Ordnance Detachments (EOD). At Lashkar Gah, the British soldiers had already replaced the US military presence and accepted full authority for the Provincial Reconstruction Team with 21 Battery RA tasked with security in the town. For the entire Battle Group the long period of training prior to deployment in which tactics had been revisited and revised was an important factor. In interviews after the tour a high number of soldiers stated that the intense training prior to arriving in Helmand saved their lives. The logistical task of delivering thousands of rounds of ammunition, vehicles and materiel from the UK to Afghanistan in 2006 was a major challenge.

In the weeks prior to the main body's arrival convoys of containers arrived in Kandahar on a daily basis, packed with Scimitars, Land Rovers, stores and rations in preparation for the Task Force. At Kabul, the UK airhead had been established since late 2001, but now both men and materiel would need to be pushed further forward to Kandahar and Helmand. In conjunction with the Permanent Joint Headquarters a huge team of specialists working in what was called the National Support Element managed the Task Force's equipment needs, flying in everything from generators and tents to vehicle spares and urgent operational requirements. The Tristar fleet flew the troops into Kabul, while C-17s ferried in stores and ammunition, sometimes straight into Kandahar. From Kabul troops were shuttled down to Camp Bastion and the headquarters base at Kandahar by C-130 Hercules, then if needed ferried by Chinook to Lashkar Gah. The extreme desert conditions and talcum powder like sand caused extra problems for the mechanics trying to keep the Hercules fleet in the air. The Tristar's capability was also challenged as the tempo of the operation increased, but the newer C17s were able to boost the strategic airlift flying in men and materiel.

At Camp Bastion both Apache and Chinook aircraft had been flown forward from Kandahar, ready to operate direct from the desert base. For the more senior ranks the relevance of the training was very important to a soldiers' morale and ability to fight with confidence. Major Chris Warhurst, the Commanding Officer of 51 Squadron Royal Engineers said: "The high level of training delivered was fundamental to our success. It gave the guys the confidence to deliver firepower and violence when required".

Men and equipment arrive to support the Task Force.

A gunner from 21 Air Defence Battery on patrol in Lashkar Gah.

British troops from 21 Battery patrol with the Afghan National Army (ANA) in Lashkar Gah.

34

//PREPARING FOR OPERATIONS
//LASHKAR GAH

Lashkar Gah is more than a thousand years old, its name means 'place of soldiers' and, with a colourful and bloody history it is no stranger to military conflict. It was here that Alexander the Great established a fortress which Genghis Khan and his forces later destroyed. A development programme of aid in the 1960s was cut short when the Soviets invaded, leaving the town with limited resources. In more recent times since the fall of the Taliban in 2001, the town has been relatively quiet but underneath the fragile peace, tribal warlords watched from the shadows and monitored the political temperature. A market town and the focal point for regional government, Lashkar Gah in early 2006 was far from stable.

Situated in the heart of Helmand Lashkar Gah is the provincial capital and as such it was the obvious location as a base for international efforts to help extend the authority of the central government as well as to facilitate development and reconstruction. American Forces had established a Provincial Reconstruction Team (PRT) in Helmand, which had been active in monitoring the security situation, liaising between opposing factions, facilitating police reform, providing intelligence to the Afghan counter narcotics authorities, and worked with other agencies providing plans for development.

In May 2006 the United States passed authority for the Provincial Reconstruction Team (PRT) in Helmand Province to the UK. At the time Lieutenant General David Richards, who commanded ISAF, said: "ISAF's main effort will be to expand the area in which the government of Afghanistan, international, and non governmental agencies can safely operate." The aim of the PRT was to operate in support of international efforts to expand the authority of the Government of Afghanistan, facilitate Security Sector Reform and enable reconstruction. In addition to military personnel, it included representatives of the Foreign and Commonwealth Office (FCO) and the Department for International Development (DFID). From the small base at Lashkar Gah the UK Provincial Reconstruction Team was based around 21 Air Defence Battery Royal Artillery with Colonel Charlie Knaggs heading the project.

Governor Doud held the post of President Karzai's government representative at Lashkar Gah in 2006. He reported to Kabul and held responsibility for the entire area with the key towns to the north being Gereshk, Sangin, Kajaki, Now Zad, Musa Qaleh and Baghran, while the major location in the south was Garmser. All of these towns had their own District Centre, which was home to the local government official. Flying the national flag, these buildings are often nothing more than old forts, but in Afghan culture they are the official face of the government and are also home to small Afghan police and army units. More importantly under the Karzai government the presence of Afghan forces at the District Centres had offered local people a feeling of security, albeit fragile, which they had sought for so long.

The planned area for development around Lashkar Gah was dubbed the 'lozenge' and the protection of the town was paramount. The urgent need to see construction start had to be balanced with the level of security. The first local contracts were to build sleeping policeman for Afghan National Police checkpoints. This vital work helped secure the town, but building vehicle checkpoints could not easily be interpreted by the international community as progress. For the gunners of 21 Air Defence Battery the first few weeks in the town would be a baptism of fire.

British soldiers from the OMLT take a break during the battle for Garmser, in which they directed and headed the ANA in their first operation.

British instructors often worked on their own with groups of Afghan soldiers.

//PREPARING FOR OPERATIONS
//AFGHAN NATIONAL ARMY

Recruits to the Afghan National Army receive their basic training in Kabul and since 2001 multi-national forces have supported training cadres to support the Government and make sure that the long term security of the country will be managed by its own national soldiers. These soldiers often finish training and go straight into combat and in order to deliver a further package of specialist training to prepare them for the front line the Operational Mentoring and Liaison Teams (OMLTs) were formed. The aim of the OMLT programme was to coach and mentor a battalion of Afghan soldiers after their graduation from their training depot. The task of generating training teams, providing administration as well as commanding the OMLT fell to 7th Parachute Regiment Royal Horse Artillery. An Afghan Army battalion is called a Kandak and the deployment of 7 Para RHA's OMLT to Helmand was to coincide with the new 3/205 ANA Brigade. While it appeared that the OMLT would be a training organisation, delivering military skills and mentoring the ANA in barracks, it quickly became apparent during a recce that the UK training teams would be required to actually deploy on operations with the ANA. While 7 Para RHA was to command the OMLT and deliver a percentage of staff. Many of the soldiers and officers who made up the OMLT came from across the British Army, resulting in a wide range of cap badges. The OMLT provided the mentoring function at all levels of command, however they worked alongside the US Logistic Support Teams (LSTs) who remained in place to facilitate pay and other logistic support to the ANA in addition to mentoring the garrison troops.

The bravery and courage of those who served with the OMLTs should not be underestimated. Often groups of just five or six British soldiers found themselves responsible for training groups of more than 50 Afghan soldiers. The mentoring was not always easy, some Afghans deserted after a week's leave and there were other teething problems. But very quickly the ANA stepped forward to support the Battle Group on operations. Sadly in the first few months of the deployment a number of ANA soldiers were killed or wounded and in June Captain Jim Philippson of 7 Para RHA, who was working with the OMLT was killed in a firefight with the Taliban. In just a couple of months these British soldiers, perhaps the unsung heroes of Helmand, had prepared and motivated the 3/205 Brigade to a level where in September 2006 an Afghan officer planned and directed, with UK assistance, the first ANA operation into Garmser in southern Helmand to reinforce the town's District Centre, after several hundred Taliban threatened to overrun it. As the operation progressed the 17 British troops who escorted the 100 strong Afghan force found themselves taking charge. The battle had commenced on the 11th September; the anniversary of the attack on the twin towers, and continued for six days.

Outnumbered and short of food the Afghans were impressive, but after their commander had been killed needed motivating to get back into the fight. The OMLT mentors moved forward and led from the front to ensure the momentum of the operation was not lost. Bombardier Sam New, of 7 Para RHA, passed a complex set of grid references to US and UK Close Air Support as he came under intense enemy fire, so intense that a round struck his radio and ended his transmission. The Afghan force defeated the Taliban and some of the OMLT personnel were decorated for their bravery.

OMLT troop commander Captain James Kennedy of 7 Para RHA recalls: "Elements of the OMLT were also deployed to the towns of Musa Quala, Now Zad, the Kajaki Dam and also in Garmser in the south of Helmand Province. All of the outstations experienced many contacts and it is safe to say that everybody utilised every ounce of training they had ever received. While out in the Combat Outposts it was an excellent opportunity to really get to know the ANA soldiers. During the various contacts great relationships were formed and when the bullets were flying the ANA would give their all in order to protect their outpost."

Fire Support Team 4 pictured at Sangin after days in the field. The team included members of 3 PARA, 7 Para RHA and the RAF Regiment.

When paratroopers deployed from Bastion on operations they carried significant amounts of ammunition and water and enough food to last them 24 hrs, although, because of the extra weight in such high temperatures, they rarely carried much food.

CHAPTERTHREE
→ **THE BATTLE FOR HELMAND**

The enemy were so near that Close Air Support was often called in to drop munitions very close to troops on the ground.

Helicopter movement was the main form of transport across Helmand.

//THE BATTLE FOR HELMAND
//3 PARA INTO ACTION

The battle for control of Helmand Province erupted within weeks of 3 PARA's arrival in southern Afghanistan. Fearing the loss of their brutal criminal narcotics business from which they controlled local people with fear and intimidation, the Taliban and their warlords made their move. Their intent quickly became apparent, they aimed to overrun the Government of Afghanistan's District centres and seize the initiative, while undermining President Karzai's plans to extend security and reconstruction in the south of the country. The Taliban wanted to send a clear message that they were in control of Helmand. Armed with heavy machine guns, rocket propelled grenades and mortars, they attacked in force.

At the operations room of the Helmand Task Force, later renamed UK Task Force, in Kandahar, the reports of firefights (contacts) with the enemy quickly became routine as staff plotted the grid references of what were called TICs (Troops in Contact). The RAF Harriers flying from the same base provided Close Air Support (CAS) to the troops on the ground while operating out of Bastion the Apache force quickly proved itself a formidable asset to operations. In addition NATO air power from fixed wing aircraft in Kabul to A10 tank busters from Bagram airbase, north of Kabul, and US Navy F-16s deployed from carriers in the Indian Ocean supported troops on the ground. Air power sent the Taliban running and in particular the psychological impact of a B1 Bomber at low level over Helmand served to unnerve the enemy.

At Baghran in the north of the Province the Taliban launched a major assault on the District Centre, followed by attacks at Musa Qaleh, Sangin and Now Zad. The Pathfinders deployed to Baghran and then Musa Qaleh along with paratroopers, Gurkhas and members of the Royal Irish Regiment. In the UK the media reported that British paratroopers had engaged in firefights with Taliban insurgents for the first time since deploying adding that Afghan soldiers and police, supported by UK forces had fought off attacks by hundreds of enemy fighters in Helmand province. It was also reported that the newly commissioned British Apache helicopters had been involved in combat operations for the first time ever. "They fired at suspected Taliban positions and offered troop support and a show of force," said Capt Drew Gibson, an Army spokesman. The tempo of the operation was now moving at a fast pace. After the initial battles a paratrooper in A Company told BBC television that it was unnerving to see the enemy running towards you with such determination. 'You just had to keep cool and make sure every shot counted, the more they came, the more we dropped. It was intense and nothing prepares you for it, you simply go into training mode and deliver everything you have been trained to do'.

As the Taliban increased their attacks it became very clear that the District Centres across Northern Helmand were in danger of falling into the hands of the enemy and the Government of Afghanistan asked the UK military for help in defending them. The strategic importance of not allowing the DCs to fall into the hands of the Taliban was paramount. A senior member of the Karzai government said it would be unacceptable to see the flag of the Taliban flying over Musa Qaleh. The plan was to reinforce the DCs with UK forces for a short period and then replace them with larger numbers of Afghan forces in order that national security troops maintained their presence.

But within a short period the Taliban started to attack British forces on a regular basis. Taliban mortars, 107mm rockets, RPGs and machine gun attacks became a daily occurrence. The Taliban rocket and mortar attacks often fell short of their target smashing into local houses injuring residents and forcing many to leave their homes. While UK forces continued to maintain overwhelming firepower, life in Musa Qaleh, Sangin and Now Zad became increasingly difficult for those soldiers who served there in extremely arduous conditions.

These remote northern outposts swiftly turned into magnets for the Taliban, who saw them as easy targets with fighting now reported at Now Zad, Musa Qaleh and Sangin, the town where the opium harvest is processed before being shipped out of the country. Sangin was always going to be a tough community to win over, as the resident farmers who relied on the poppy had been encouraged by the Taliban to believe that that the UK was there to destroy their income. It was at Musa Qaleh and Sangin that some of the bloodiest fighting took place. After an intense attack on the District Centre at Sangin, A Company were sent in to restore stability. Landing by helicopter a mile and a half outside Sangin the company, made its way without incident to the government compound and evacuated the wounded Afghans. They then set up makeshift fortifications and 'sangars' - sandbagged firing positions - made themselves at home as best they could and waited for a week while nothing at all happened. Then one night, the sky erupted as rocket-propelled grenades, Chinese-made 107mm rockets and AK47 automatic rifle rounds thumped into the District Centre from houses overlooking the British base. Paratroopers, many of whom were wearing only shorts because of the extreme heat, swiftly donned body armour and responded in kind with heavy machine-gun fire that eventually silenced the Taliban.

41

The District Centre at Musa Qaleh.

The fighting was so close that bayonets were often fixed.

//THE BATTLE FOR HELMAND

//THE DISTRICT CENTRES

Across the country the Government of Afghanistan manages local towns through what are known as District Centres. Flying the national flag, these buildings are often nothing more than civic compounds, but in Afghan culture they are the official face of the government and are also home to small Afghan police and army units. More importantly under the Karzai government the presence of Afghan forces at the District Centres had offered local people a feeling of security, albeit fragile, which they had sought for so long. A tense form of stability resulted and ensured that the District Centres had a vital role to play in the bigger strategic plan to deliver a safe and secure environment in order to allow reconstruction to take place across Helmand. The District Centres (DCs) are the equivalent of local council buildings in the UK, but there are few trappings of high office, no running water or conference rooms. The only indicator of the building's importance is the high mud wall, which surrounds the official courtyard of all the DCs and in some cases the ageing iron gates which mark the entrance.

As British forces started to arrive in Helmand in April 2006, The Taliban launched their offensive and attacked the District Centres in what was a clear plan to seize control of the buildings and undermine the Government and its authority across Helmand. As the Taliban increased their attacks it became very clear that the District Centres across Northern Helmand were in danger of falling into the hands of the enemy and the Government of Afghanistan asked the UK military for help in defending them. To allow these District Centres to fall to the enemy would give them a major publicity coup and a strategic victory to the enemy.

In late May British troops reinforced the District Centres, which were also known as the Platoon Houses. Companies were garrisoned in these civic compounds from where they mounted patrols into the local town. D (Royal Gurkha Rifles) Company deployed to Now Zad, while A Company went into Sangin and C Company to Gereshk leaving B Company to support ops across the Province before going into Sangin. Eventually all 3 PARA companies were to spend several weeks in Sangin. At Musa Qaleh, after the Pathfinders, the Danes were later replaced by The Royal Irish, Paratroopers from 3 PARA and specialists from across the Battle Group. But as the Taliban attacked the bases their in-direct weapons (which were mortars and rockets) often fell short hitting local property and local people. While troops from the Battle Group manned these Centres their commander Lt Col Stuart Tootal was also planning for operations across Helmand to broaden security in the area.

It appeared that by attacking the DCs and forcing UK forces to protect them the Taliban had made a clever tactical move that was to fix UK forces and reduce their freedom of movement across Helmand. Whether in fact their military commanders planned this or they simply saw the DCs as a 'target of opportunity' may never be known. The Government of Afghanistan feared that if the DCs fell into Taliban control the insurgents would score a significant psychological victory and risk the collapse of future security across the country. For the Taliban their flawed intent was to cost them many lives.

43

The then Defence Secretary John Reid is briefed by staff officers at the UK Task Force headquarters.

The operations room was manned day and night with senior officers monitoring events in Helmand and other areas of Afghanistan.

//THE BATTLE FOR HELMAND
//COMMAND AND CONTROL

The UK Task Force, deployed to southern Afghanistan, to replace a US force. British troops first took responsibility for the Provincial Reconstrucion Team (PRT) at a ceremony in Lashkar Gah. Then later in the summer NATO took command of operations in southern Afghanistan under the umbrella of ISAF, the International Security and Assistance Force, which was commanded by a British officer, Lieutenant General David Richards. Each region of the country reported to a regional command, with the UK working to Regional Command South, which was based in Kandahar. Initially called the Helmand Task Force, the name was later switched to UK Task Force. (UKTF). The UKTF headquarters was the focal point of information, planning and decision making in support of the 3 PARA Battle Group. Specialist staff officers made sure that all equipment and materiel the force needed from ammunition stocks to medical resources and urgent operational requirements, was delivered as quickly as possible to maintain the tempo of operations across the Area of Operation (AOR). Liaison officers representing units deployed at Camp Bastion updated staff about current activity, availability and planning to ensure that everyone working in the headquarters was aware of the latest information. Initially based at Lashkar Gah the headquarters moved to Kandahar, where Regional Command South, the formation which the UKTF reported was located. British forces arrived in theatre immediately prior to Operation Mountain Thrust, an offensive operation planned by the US Commander aimed at setting suitable conditions for the transfer of authority to NATO forces. Tucked away in an unmarked area of the base, the UKTF headquarters building was not easy to find and from the outside looked like an abandoned store. But inside rows of desks identified the various functions; while in a darkened area of the building the operations room was the beating heart of the headquarters, always working and ready to react to situations and contacts on the ground. Prior to the arrival of the headquarters in Helmand the Taliban had maintained a clear influence and by April 2006 held power and sway across the Province. The UKTF faced a huge challenge in order to bring about firstly, security and secondly, to win the 'hearts and minds' campaign. The commander of the force, Brigadier Ed Butler, had very little sleep in the first months of the deployment as he looked for an opportunity to deliver what the military term an 'effect'. This would in turn deliver security and support the hearts and minds campaign to allow reconstruction to commence. But the arrival of the Taliban in large numbers was set to delay the security phase and no doubt impact on the development plan. His strategy in gaining an effect was simple in that he planned to fix and if necessary destroy the Taliban in order to provide a secure environment that would allow government agencies to organise a programme of reconstruction. But his difficulty was in getting that message to farmers and local people who were being heavily intimidated by the enemy across northern Helmand. The Taliban had tried to stir up a storm against UK forces by telling people that the UK was going to destroy the poppy and when that failed they threatened death to anyone who spoke to British troops. In the town of Musa Qaleh the Taliban executed a woman and her son in the street as a demonstration of what might happen to others.

Fixed wing aircraft were often called in to neutralise enemy attacks.

As well as RAF Harriers, NATO aircraft including this US Marine F18 supported UK troops on the ground.

//THE BATTLE FOR HELMAND
//216 (AA) SIGNAL SQUADRON

The Squadron began deploying to southern Afghanistan in preparation for an eight month long tour. The unit deployed in its primary role of supplying command and communications life support to the 16 Brigade Main Headquarters which was initially in Lashkar Gah, while the rest of the Squadron deployed to the four corners of Helmand and Kandahar Provinces attached to various units to fulfil key roles in support of the operation. For all concerned Helmand was an operational tour like no other.

Lance Corporal 'Sea Horse' Telford was attached to the Estonian Rear Link Detachment and deployed to Garmser as the Estonians cleared the town of Taliban insurgents. The tour is one he will never forget, he said: "The language barrier caused many a humorous moment especially when we stopped and had time to chill out; they did not appreciate my British sense of humour and sarcasm. I was impressed with their skills and drills, especially their 'no-nonsense' attitude towards their task. We were constantly surrounded by fighting between Taliban and the Afghan National Police (ANP) and twice found ourselves on the receiving end of Small Arms and RPG fire, which resulted in three Estonians being wounded from RPGs being used in the 'Air-burst' role. However it did not seem to affect their performance or enthusiasm to take on the enemy. I was fortunate enough to experience Close Air Support being brought in on enemy positions. It was a great opportunity to get out of camp and to apply my trade under immense pressure. I was living out my bergan, using my Bowman HF man-pack and TacSat both of which I had learned to use in Helmand without any previous training. It was an incredible experience that I will never ever forget."

Signaller Shyrane found himself attached to the Provincial Reconstruction Team. He recalls: "Being a driver I never thought I would get the opportunity to serve in the Provincial Reconstruction Team, but in early February, 22 of us from 216 were packed off for pre-deployment training with 21 Air Assault Gibraltar Battery, Royal Artillery. Arriving in Afghanistan with our new skills and newly forged friendships we began the hard work of establishing ourselves in Lashkar Gah. I was, at first, very weary as it was my first tour in the Army, but as we started patrolling on the ground in Lashkar Gah our nerves soon faded away as we started gelling as a team. Our job was to provide Force Protection as well as providing the security to enable aid and reconstruction work. We soon found the locals coming up to thank us, you could not help notice the huge smiles on the faces of the kids, which proved to us just how important and worthwhile our work in Afghanistan was. One of my most memorable moments, was our first 'contact' in Garmser.

"I was at first worried at how I would react, but within split seconds I was concentrating on doing my best for the lads around me. We were taking loads of RPGs and heavy machine gun fire, but the guys were focussed and took the fight to the Taliban aggressively, Signalle Guyton our intrepid female hammering it down with the .50 Cal. The morale was through the roof".

Lance Corporal 'Asda' Summerfield was sent to 3 PARA as part of a Rear Link Detachment. He said : "In June I deployed with Signaller 'First Tour' Perkins and Signaller 'Fag Break' Mazzone to join Lt Hollingshead's 12 Platoon D Company 2 Royal Gurkha Regiment as a Rear Link team to Sangin to secure a platoon house. We flew from Camp Bastion to COP Robinson and then deployed into Sangin town to secure the ANP station. We stayed there for a few days before we were pulled out back to COP Robinson due to a high threat state. We continued to carry out patrolling tasks from the base over the next couple of weeks with the aim of establishing contact with the locals and to try identifying the Taliban threat. It was a brilliant opportunity and excellent experience to get out on the ground, patrolling in the infantry role alongside the Gurkhas and demonstrate that 216 Sqaudron could also step up and take on an infantry role as well as the making sure that the communications provided were, as always, of a high standard. I will remember Helmand for the unique experience of living and working shoulder to shoulder with the Gurkhas, but also the way in which we all pulled together when things were really becoming tricky. Over the two months our skills were tested almost daily by the Taliban and not once did we give an inch."

Paratroopers fill sandbags to reinforce their base against attack.

Captain Chris Hitchens, front right, and the men of 8 Platoon, C Company inside Sangin.

//INSIDE THE DISTRICT CENTRES

The District Centres or Platoon Houses as they became known had no home comforts. These buildings which represented the Government of Afghanistan had no running water, no sanitation, almost no furniture and offered little protection against enemy attack. For those Paratroopers, Rangers, Gurkhas and specialist units of 16 Air Assault Brigade who were among the first into these buildings, the dust and smell will remain with them for a long time. The intensity of enemy attack prevented anyone from relaxing, from the minute soldiers arrived at a District Centres they remained alert and ready. The constant periods of action and lack of sleep was dehabiltating, but the motivation of the Battle Group was so high that they soldiers simply rose above the challenge to engage the Taliban at every opportunity.

Those who served in the Platoon Houses included all three rifle companies of 3 PARA, D Company of 2 RGR together with significant attachments from Mortars and Fire Support Teams of 7 Para RHA, 216 Signal and 51 Squadron Royal Engineers and A Company RRF, who also reinforced 3 PARA and were garrisoned at Now Zad. All spent substantial periods of time operating from the confines of the municpal compounds of Sangin, Now Zad, Musa Qaleh and Kajaki, and experienced considerable action against the Taliban. There was no air conditioning and at night the air was thick with mosquitos. The issue roll mat provided some comfort against the rock hard ground and the mosquito nets were excellent. Later as the tour progressed oil drums were converted into toilets and conditions improved slighlty every day. But in the first three weeks there was little opportunity for sleep for those deployed at Sangin.The first paratroopers at the Distirct Centre worked around the clock filling sandbags, building sangars and trenches – all the time protected by colleagues . After two weeks of snatching 30 minutes sleep at a time the soldiers were shattered. Following each attack more repairs were carried out and eventually a semblance of order permitted a few hours of sleep at a time, but only during hours of daylight as the inevitable attacks started after dark.

There was simply not enough hard cover to allow those who needed sleep to be under shelter. Day and night paratroopers who were due on guard slept at the feet of the colleagues in shell scarapes, alongside mortar barrels and heavy machine guns, all getting used to sleeping one minute and fighting the next. The defensive positions were constantly checked to make sure they were robust and capable of withstanding an RPG or an accurate burst of Heavy Machine Gun fire. They were kept tidy and clutter-free like any other living space apart from the pile of spare ammunition kept to hand and the stockpiles of water. Fresh water was used sparingly; only for drinking and cleaning teeth – washing was conducted in a nearby canal, covered by fire from defensive positions. Living conditions as an issue paled into insignificance compared to the near-constant threat to life and limb.

Many soldiers from 3 PARA took part in contacts against the Taliban. Prior to the Platoon Houses being established - Op MUTAY in the Now Zad area had provided some with their first ever combat experience.

In Sangin there was a period of relentless enemy attack which included RPGs, small arms and 107mm rockets. The enemy focussed their attack at Sangin on the sangar and the prominent tower in which 3 PARA housed a Fire Support Group of mixed machine guns and snipers. Throughout the early deployment of 3 PARA, the tower and central building took numerous direct hits from RPGs, small arms and a 107mm rocket. While a number of 107mm rockets had impacted against the compound's outer wall, one struck the tower on the evening of 1st July killing two soldiers and an interpreter and wounding another six men.

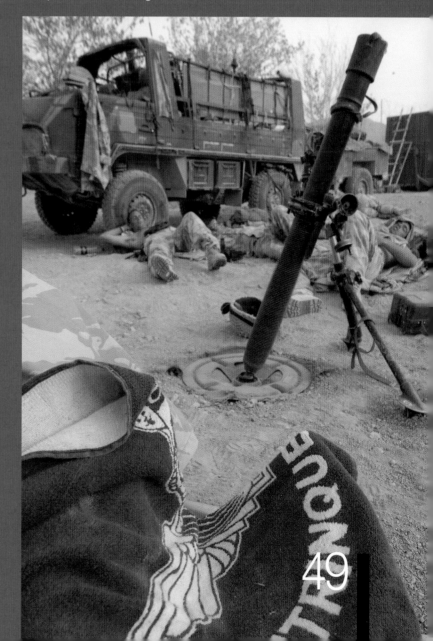

C/Sgt Mick Whordley enjoys a five minute break inside the Sangin District Centre with paratroopers.

Private Nixon, nearest the camera, is pictured during an operation near Sangin.

50

//THE BATTLE FOR HELMAND
//SANGIN

The town of Sangin lies in the Helmand valley and is notorious as the staging post for the packing of opium on its journey out of Afghanistan. It claims to have a population of 12,000 people, but many of these live in isolated communities away from the main town. Situated north of Lashkar Gah, Sangin was, and still is, of strategic importance to the Taliban. In early 2006 they were the police, the judge and jury in Sangin, they paid the farmers for their annual poppy harvest and it was the Taliban who exploited the community to extreme. After years of rule local people initially trusted the Taliban rather than the UK Task Force. Sangin was always regarded as the most anti-western town in Helmand Province and this may have been due to the vicious reign of terror inflicted on the community who faced public humiliation and possible death if they disobeyed the Taliban and their warlords.

When Coalition forces entered Afghanistan in 2001 a number of US troops deployed to the south, with the main force going to Kandahar. US Special Forces worked hard to establish a 'hearts and minds' foothold in Helmand but their lack of numbers prevented progress. The area is extremely volatile and in July 2005 a United Nations convoy of six vehicles came under attack by Taliban forces several miles south of the town, thankfully they all escaped. The fields around Sangin are red with poppies in the growing season and the entire town has been forced by the Taliban to grow the plant. The $multi-million opium business fills the Taliban's war chest, but delivers little revenue to the town. Once the Taliban is defeated the Government of Afghanistan has indicated that its main effort will focus on encouraging new crops, which will assist the Afghan economy and provide financial reward for the local farmers.

51

Above left, paratroopers prepare to board a Chinook during operations at Now Zad. A paratrooper passes the remain of a bombed house at Now Zad, which looks very similar to Sangin.

Dusty and battle hardened paratroopers pictured at Now Zad.

//THE BATTLE FOR HELMAND
//NOW-ZAD

Now Zad is situated to the far west of Helmand Province and like neighbouring Musa Qaleh and Sangin offered little comfort to the local community. No hard roads, poor almost primitive living conditions, limited power and water and a society where childhood ends at an early age with little or no education. The local economy was based on arms smuggling and limited profits handed back to them by the Taliban from the opium trade. The District Compound was situated in the centre of the main bazaar with civilian buildings all around. While preliminary operations had identified the need to focus on hearts and minds in Now Zad, the town unfortunately suffered from a heavy Coalition air strike just as UK troops were arriving. As a result the local community were suspicious and the Taliban appeared to have a clear hold over local people. The Gurkhas of D Company of 3 PARA, deployed from the UK during the second week of April and 10 Platoon was deployed to Now Zad in June to reinforce the District Centre.

Their time in Now Zad was busy with numerous contacts. Then in July, 11 Platoon deployed to the town under the command of Major Dan Rex and the Platoon Commander, Lt Angus Mathers, to conduct a relief-in-place with 10 Platoon and maintain the defensive position located in the District Compound. As the platoon disembarked from the Chinooks and established an all-round defensive position on the Helicopter Landing Site (HLS), a burst of fire was heard to the east and what was believed to be mortar fire. The Gurkhas were caught in the open ground, but immediately, a 3 PARA Fire Support Group (FSG) returned fire with Javelin and mortars, destroying the enemy firing point. The engagement last six hours with three major air strikes being called in. Later, the Royal Regiment of Fusiliers who had arrived in Helmand to support the Battle Group deployed a company to Now Zad to take over from D Company Royal Gurkha Rifles.

RAF Harriers were called into support operations south of Gereshk at Garmser where the Afghan National Army mounted their first mission. Right, a member of 7 Para RHA looks down on the river running from the Kajacki dam.

A paratrooper of C Company pictured in Gereshk.

//THE BATTLE FOR HELMAND
//GERESHK AND KAJAKI

These locations, one in the south and one in the north, were both strategically important to the UK Task Force operation. Gereshk is the gateway to the southeast and it was from here that Afghan National Army (ANA) operations could be pushed forward to Garmser. The town of Gereshk was initially home to C Company and one of the first and most intense firefights took place just south of the village of Zumbelay. The incident, which received world wide press coverage, took place in early June, when the company commander Major Blair took a patrol to the village. The Taliban had set a trap and attempted to cut off the patrol and kill them. But after a ferocious series of firefights they fought their way out and retuned to Gereshk. By August 2006, the District Centre in Garmser was increasingly being attacked by the Taliban, resulting in the first ANA planned and executed operation, albeit directed by just 17 British soldiers from the OMLT (Operational Mentoring and Liaison Team). The Kajaki Dam is at the head of the Sangin Valley and Helmand River.

This hydro-electric water source was built between 1955 and 1975 and was financed jointly by the Republic of Afghanistan and the USA (USAID). But the American input was abandoned when the Soviets invaded the country. In 2006, the reconstruction plan for the dam listed the replacement of a large turbine and repair of the facility as a priority to provide power to two million Afghans. However, the intense level of fighting left little opportunity for reconstruction work. The dam will be a major part of the development of Helmand and as such the name Kajaki will feature heavily in both military and civil planning in the years ahead. For 3 PARA the name Kajaki will always be associated with Cpl Mark Wright. It was while patrolling this area that Cpl Wright and his men ran into a minefield, despite his own critical injuries he tragically died when he repeatedly tried to rescue a wounded comrade. He was later awarded the George Cross.

Afghan National Army and British troops pictured during operations in Garmser which were mounted from Gereshk.

The Fire Support Teams were able to offer the spectrum of Joint Fires (Mortars, Artillery, AH and CAS in support of the Rifle Companies.

Cpl Ryan Rogers became the first British soldier to fire Javelin on operations.

//THE BATTLE FOR HELMAND
//FIRE SUPPORT GROUPS

The Machine Gun and Anti Tank platoons were re-organised for the deployment to southern Afghanistan into four FSGs (Fire Support Groups) which were able to deliver mounted or dismounted support to the Rifle Companies. The FSGs provided static firepower in the form of .50 calibre and the General Purpose Machine Gun (GPMG) in the Sustained Fire (SF) role as well as Javelin and Milan missiles at Sangin, Kajaki, and Now Zad. They also carried out manoeuvre operations in their own right as convoy escorts in the WMIK role (Land Rover based gun teams) and thirdly as in the more direct support to companies or to Battle Group in the dismounted role on operations.

The FSG concept was extremely flexible and the teams changed constantly due to Wounded in Action (WiA), leave and compassionate cases, all of which happened on a regular basis. The use of Direct Fire Heavy Weapons proved their worth time and time again. The comfort of having something organic (in the form of a larger calibre weapon) than the Taliban in order to respond to incoming fire is not to be underestimated. Both physically and psychologically, the direct fire assets of the FSG had a devastating effect on the enemy. The surveillance and targeting ability of the Command Launch Unit (CLU) (part of the Javelin system) was also excellent. The speed and weight of fire of the mounted FSG's was proven in particular during the highly publicised Zumbelay contact. Good training and effective WMIK contact

drills and the ability to perform a hasty firebase were proven when Capt Mackenzie's and Sgt McMellon's FSG engaged numerous enemy and protected a substantial ground element, whilst under fire from as close as 100 metres from substantial enemy groupings. The FSG managed to neutralise a section plus formation including RPG gunners and a Dshk team. Pte 'Ginge' Carroll of the Machine Guns managed to fire five boxes of .50 calibre, and contributed significantly to winning the firefight. This is just one of many incidents that took place at close quarters in a close and savage environment.

The FSGs also suffered a number of injuries during the operaton. Pte Brown and Evans of the Machine Guns and Pte Scott of the Anti-Tank Platoon were wounded in Sangin from an RPG round. Cpl Pearson of the ATK platoon lost a leg in the Kajaki mine strike incident and Pte Harvey risked his own life to give immediate first aid to Cpl Hale.

Corporal Ryan Rogers wrote himself into military history when he became the first soldier in the British Army to fire the Javelin on operations. During a particularly fierce engagement with the Taliban in which paratroopers at Sangin were under intense fire from an enemy fortified position Cpl Rogers moved forward and fired the weapon to silence the Taliban. He was commended for his action in a commendation from the force commander Brigadier Butler.

The GPMG in the SF role and the Heavy Machine Gun were among the support provided by the FSGs.

MACHINE GUN 7.62mm
BL.65 A2814
1005-13-10

Mortar bunker with two members of the crew looking exhausted.

The Mortar Platoon pictured in full throttle.

//THE BATTLE FOR HELMAND
//MORTAR PLATOON - 3 PARA

The Mortar Platoon was involved in some way in almost every operation undertaken by the Battle Group. The final totals for ammunition expended was 6,578 rounds fired, of which 4,245 were High Explosive (HE). Nearly 900 separate fire missions were recorded, making the Mortar Fire Controllers in the platoon some of the most combat experienced since World War Two. The nature of the contacts in many cases pushed their skills to the limits. Fire missions were called in to within 40-50 metres of friendly troops engaged in firefights with the Taliban. Such was the confidence between the MFCs and the rifle companies that this became routine. The speed of the mortar detachments resulted in fire being delivered within two minutes of a fire mission being called.

Cpl Mark Wright (pictured right), the Bravo MFC for A Company was killed in action on 6th September in Kajaki as a result of being hit by an anti personnel mine. He died trying to save the lives of two other paratroopers who had been severely injured while patrolling into an unmarked minefield. Despite being severely injured himself, he continued to reassure all those trapped in the minefield for a number of hours, and it was his command

and control that ensured the safe extraction of all of the injured. Unfortunately Cpl Wright could not hold on long enough to reach the hospital, and he passed away before he could get to hospital. Several members of the platoon were also injured during the tour. CSgt Bell broke his leg whilst jumping from a CH47 that was lifting off to avoid incoming RPG fire. Despite this, he persevered, calling in fire that destroyed a number of Taliban strongholds and disrupted numerous attempted counter attacks against UK forces. Cpl Cartwright was injured when a 107mm rocket attack hit Sangin. Despite being moved back to the UK for treatment, he returned to theatre and managed to deploy on the last operation to Sangin. Cpl Roberts was shot in the shoulder whilst on patrol, also in Sangin. Pte Prosser, having only just rejoined the platoon, was hit by shrapnel during the same mine incident that killed Cpl Wright.

Mortar team pictured at Sangin.

Cpl Curnow, Pte Phillips, L/Cpl Stephens and Pte Evans of 2 Platoon pictured inside Sangin.

Paratroopers from C Company pictured during the heat of a firefight.

CHAPTERFOUR
→ FACE TO FACE WITH THE TALIBAN

The battle at Now Zad in which paratroopers experienced the commitment of the Taliban to fight.

A Company WMIK Land Rovers pictured during Op MUTAY.

//FACE TO FACE WITH THE TALIBAN
//FIRST ACTION

The 3 PARA Battle Group had quickly made its presence felt across Helmand, deploying routine patrols and mounting security assessments. But the threat against the District Houses continued with growing numbers of Taliban reported to have moved into the region. In late May, the battalion's fighting companies and supporting arms were deployed to secure the District Centres at Now Zad, Gereshk, Sangin and Musa Qaleh. Troops were also deployed to Kajaki to protect the dam. At the end of the month planning was underway for a search and cordon operation at Now Zad where intelligence had indicated that enemy forces were forming in numbers. The Patrols platoon and the Gurkhas of D Company were already in the District Centre providing valuable reports.

On 4th June, A Company 3 PARA was tasked as part of a Battle Group level operation to mount a cordon and search of a walled compound to the east of Now Zad. The compound was situated in a 'bocage' area characterised by numerous orchards, multiple, and often inter connecting, high walled compounds and irrigation channels. The immediate area was flat though the ground rose sharply about 1.5 kilometres to the east of the target compound. Visibility on the ground was about 60-70 metres and foot movement was severely restricted, and canalised, by the high walls and the compounds. Fortunately the company had deployed with ladders. Intelligence was scant but the company had been warned that there were Taliban in the area. The Patrols Platoon and Gurkha elements were already in the Platoon House in Now Zad and were tasked with the outer cordon to the west and east respectively. They deployed from the Platoon House when the Chinooks were ten minutes out. The Gurkhas were to link up with A Company Group and deliver the District Chief and some Afghan National Police (ANP) to assist with the search and ensure the operation had an Afghan lead. A Company Group was to land in four Chinooks immediately to the north and south west of the target compound in order to achieve an immediate seal on that location. The Support Helicopter packet was preceded by two Apaches (AH) who arrived five minutes earlier. L Hr was 1210 hrs on 4th June.

At L Hour, the three Chinooks landed on, two to the north with Company Tactical headquarters (Tac), the Royal Engineers and 2 Platoon. The other Chinook landed 400m to the west since it could not land in the pre designated Landing Site. The fourth Chinook held the Commanding Officer's Tac and Airborne Reaction Force drawn from the Support Company Fire Support Group and remained airborne as the Airborne Command and Control Centre (ABCCC). The AH provided top cover.

As soon as the helicopters landed the Taliban attacked, demonstrating the speed of the enemy reaction. These contacts were centred on the Patrols Platoon, 1 Platoon and the Gurkhas to the north and were all independent engagements. Within the cordon location enemy fire was coming in at the height of the walls, ensuring for A Company that it was ineffective and almost certainly not directed at any elements within the inner cordon, although still 'threatening' in contact terms.

Simultaneously the Gurkhas were ambushed by a similar grouping to the north and a firefight erupted with the Gurkhas accounting for a number of enemy kills. After 30 minutes the Gurkhas extracted to the west and moved to the 'Shrine' area to the south west of Now Zad. At this time 1 Platoon came under fire as they landed and after a brief firefight moved swiftly to their inner cordon location to the south of the target compound. Within the compound the search was initiated and was to continue until late in the afternoon. The Patrols Platoon moved south from their initial contact location and after 30 minutes were attacked again by another similar grouping. This firefight was sporadic but spanned two hours. Throughout all this activity Apache provided outstanding service in suppressing or destroying the Taliban at very close proximity to 3 PARA troops. The Interim Light Anti-Tank weapon, a 94mm shoulder held rocket, proved useful in indicating targets for engagement by Apache. It became increasingly clear that the nature of the terrain was no place for vehicles without accompanying infantry and so the Patrols Platoon was ordered to move south west to a more open area.

At about 1245 hrs, the fourth Chinook landed with the CO's Tac and the Fire Support Group in light mode. Sporadic firing continued for most of the afternoon while the search progressed. During this time intelligence was received indicating the location of a Taliban leader some 4-500 metres to the west of the compound. Very quickly 2 Platoon with the Forward Observation Officer and Forward Air Control Party (Fire Support Team) was deployed to sweep this area and if possible capture this figure. This was an extremely difficult task since it entailed a fighting patrol going out to the location though very close country to try and locate a fleeting and unidentified personality. At about 1530 hrs the Platoon deployed and was engaged shortly thereafter. There followed an extremely well controlled platoon level action involving efficient fire and movement, excellent use of the snipers and fantastic support both from Apache and USAF A10s. A number of Taliban were killed and at about 1630 hrs the Platoon was ordered to recover back into the cordon. Still under fire, the Platoon's Fire Support Team, commanded by Capt Armstrong RHA, directed the A10 tank buster back into action which, at 50 yards from 2 Platoon, delivered devastating fire to the source of enemy fire; enemy fire from that location ceased.

To the East of the cordon the Fire Support Group and snipers identified a wheel barrow being pushed 'at speed' north up the Wadi. They moved to interdict and found a badly wounded Afghan in the barrow. He was brought into the cordon and treated by the Regimental Medical Officer and medics. The wounded man was then extracted with the Company and treated at Camp Bastion. As the situation continued 1 Platoon heard Pashtu voices near to their location to the south of the Cordon. The Platoon identified Taliban approaching the cordon and, following a warning, engaged a two man RPG team killing them both.

A Gurkha from D Company in Now Zad.

It was extremely difficult for those on the ground to identify the location of the fire. The Patrols Platoon had been engaged by a group of about ten fighters armed with rocket propelled grenades and Kalashnikovs and they continued to rain firepower into the inner cordon area. Fire was returned and at least three Taliban kills claimed. Apache was brought on to target the enemy rapidly by the Forward Air Controller with the Patrols and the Taliban were engaged with 30mm.

There followed an engagement, again amongst the orchards and compounds, with fierce exchanges of fire and grenades at very close proximity. At least a further two enemy fighters were killed in this action. This continued until about 1630 hrs when Apache returned to station and the fire died down. The firefight by 1 Platoon had displayed yet again the sheer quality of The Parachute Regiment's junior officers, Sergeants, Corporals and Toms (Parachute Regiment nickname for Private soldiers). Their calmness and professionalism under heavy fire was quite excellent. At 1700hrs with the search complete and the Patrols back into the cordon the time had come to extract. The search had uncovered drugs, small arms ammunition and firearms. The Company Group then moved beneath the cover of two Apaches and two RAF GR7 Harriers, and headed east to a large Wadi where it was extracted in four Chinooks.

Above, mobile phone pictures capture the action during the operation. Below, the fourth Chinook which carried the CO's Tactical Headquarters.

An Royal Military Police soldier provides cover for A Company soldiers as they move across open ground.

Members of B Company at Now Zad in search of the Taliban, left, who ruled the town before 3 PARA arrived.

Paratroopers pictured in a street as they wait for the call into action. This was Close Quarter Fighting at its most lethal.

Captain Jim Philippson RHA, below, who served with the OMLT, was the first member of the UK Task Force to be killed in 2006.

//FACE TO FACE WITH THE TALIBAN
//CLOSE QUARTER FIGHTING

By late June 2006, the security situation in the town of Sangin had deteriorated significantly. The District Chief and his Afghan Police guard were under constant attack from Taliban insurgents. At one point, when the District Centre was under frequent attacks by day and by night, it looked as though the town may have been overrun by Taliban fighters. Following a request for help by the District Chief, A Company Group was called upon to air assault into the town and secure the District Centre, and facilitate the extraction of wounded Afghans. Briefly, the scheme of manoeuvre was for the Company to land on an Helicopter Landing Site (HLS) next to the Helmand River, approximately two kilometres from the District Centre and patrol to the compound before occupying it and extracting the wounded. Having landed at dawn without incident, the first elements of the Company reached the compound through the morning haze after an hour, and much to everyone's surprise, got into the compound without a fight. The wounded were quickly identified and treated. Then using traditional airborne initiative, members of the Company Group, begged, borrowed and stole bricks, planks of wood and boxes, to fortify the District Centre against further attacks. The hasty preparation was soon completed including the digging in of a mortar line of two barrels, preparation of GPMG SF (Sustained Fire) positions, and the siting of Claymores. For a week nothing happened.

Then one night in late June the stillness of the cool night air was shattered with the sound of RPGs fizzing overhead and 7.62mm rounds cracking and thumping into the sangars. Muzzle flashes lit up the enemy positions in and around the various hardened mud and brick buildings that lie across the wadi in front of the District Centre. Around the compound paratroopers sprang to life, responding heavily with accurate .50cal, GPMG SF, mortars and rifle fire. It was a brief but nevertheless exhausting engagement. Afterwards as they took post, refilled magazines, refreshed their water bottles and adjusted their improvised defensive positions on the rooftops, nobody knew that this engagement would set the tone for Company Group and Battle Group operations in the weeks and months to come. Over the following nights the Taliban repeatedly attacked the base with all the weapons available to them. On only one occasion did they undertake a frontal assault on a narrow front to try and seize the compound. This was however directly at a sangar manned with a GPMG and duly repulsed. Members of the Company became used to leaping from filling sandbags straight into stand to positions, often in shorts and body armour only due to the oppressive heat. Sadly on the night of 1st July the Taliban used a 107 mm rocket which struck the roof of the fire support tower, killing Corporal Thorpe and Lance Corporal Hashimi from 14 Signal Regiment and a local national employed as an interpreter.

The GPMG in the mounted SF Sustained Fire role.

A few days later B Company began a relief in place with A Company. As this took place on 4th July, 1 Platoon were ambushed as they moved in to secure the HLS for helicopters to land in Sangin. Sadly Private Damien Jackson was fatally wounded in the ensuing battle.

Fighting intensified for B Company with A Company returning to Sangin for one week in mid-July, and for a third and final time beginning in the last few days of July. The purpose of this stay was threefold. First to provide protection to the Royal Engineers who were conducting work to improve the field fortifications of the Sangin District Centre, and in particular the HLS. Second to disrupt enemy activity, identifying and destroying them where possible. Finally to reassure the local population of the Coalition's long term intent to develop and reconstruct Afghanistan. The third stay lasted a total of 35 days of which 31 days involved contact with the enemy as the situation deteriorated and fighting grew more intense. A patrol into the area of the town on 27th July sensed the uneasiness of the local population, and as it returned towards the District Centre everything went quiet, locals shut their shops, and people disappeared. Pte McKinley spotted two gunmen on a roof as the patrol crossed the wadi, and immediately engaged them. This started a contact which involved several enemy firing points with multiple RPGs and AK47 variant weapons. Pte Edwards was wounded in the initial exchanges, and immobilised in the wadi with a broken femur. Cpl Bryan Budd led his section forward to push the enemy back, and personally dispatched two enemy taking cover in a nearby building with grenades and rifle fire. Pte Edwards was treated and evacuated thanks to members of D Squadron, the Household Cavalry Regiment.

Paratrooper Damien Jackson of 1 Platoon who was killed at Sangin.

Pte McKinley who had spotted the enemy initially and started the engagement was also wounded with shrapnel and evacuated from the scene. The following day the deputy Chief of Police indicated his desire to remove his personal guard from the Afghan National Police contingent that was co-located next to the District Centre. This was the first indication of the pressures on the police that were fracturing their loyalties. Unlike elsewhere in Helmand province the ANP in Sangin declined to wear uniform because they feared Taliban attack. Over the following days the loyalty of the police became more dubious. The Deputy Chief fled the area on 2nd August, and on 7th August a split emerged among the six remaining policemen with three leaving. The remainder soon left rather than accept the Coalition protection that was offered to them.

On the ground the situation continued to deteriorate. 1 Platoon had further contact with the enemy on patrol on 30th July, and 2 Platoon were ambushed at close quarters in urban terrain on 31st July miraculously not sustaining any casualties. The enemy continued to attack the District Centre by day and night with small arms fire, RPGs and 107mm rockets. Thankfully the only one that hit failed to explode, with the remainder overshooting to the south. The Engineers working on improving the perimeter were frequent targets for attack, although they often could not hear the enemy fire over the noise of the plant engines. Despite their best efforts the enemy emerged worse in every engagement, and it was always only a matter of time in the initial contact until superior firepower, marksmanship and training tipped the balance in the Company's favour.

In the middle of August the attacks against the District Centre resorted to increased use of stand off weapons as closer attacks were easily defeated. Enemy seen moving into position with weapons were identified and killed on 15th and 16th of August. On 18th August the enemy introduced an 82 mm mortar team into the area which landed five rounds inside the District Centre perimeter during their first attack. Mortar attacks continued in a similar fashion before last light on 19th, 20th, and 21st August before this mortar team was destroyed on 22nd August. A combination of luck and aggressive counter-mortar fire meant that the Company Group did not sustain any casualties.

On 17th August 1 Platoon were on a patrol south of the HLS, supported by a Scimitar and Spartan from the Household Cavalry. The armoured vehicles were in the open area of the wadi, whereas the platoon were in the close country south of the HLS, characterised by high fields of corn and maize, narrow tracks and irrigation ditches. The platoon began to detain two individuals who were clearly reporting on the patrol's movements, but as they did so spotted seven enemy moving along a track with weapons.

The enemy saw the platoon almost at the same time, and a fierce engagement began. 1 Platoon conducted a platoon attack preceded by mortar fire onto the enemy position forcing them to withdraw. With nothing further to be gained, Lt Farmer took the decision to withdraw north back towards the District Centre. However, in the opening exchange of fire the two prisoners were killed by enemy fire, a fact that the Taliban appeared to be unaware of. As they received reinforcements the enemy began a determined pursuit of 1 Platoon, clearly intent on recovering the prisoners. 1 Platoon were engaged by a second group of enemy on the other side of the canal that runs north south across the area. This position was suppressed, and the Platoon began to move towards the wadi. The HCR vehicles in the wadi had been manoeuvring to get into positions of fire support, but had not engaged due to the difficulties of target identification through thick vegetation. As they manoeuvred the Spartan lost a track and became immobilised. 1 Platoon were forced to put in a snap ambush to deal with the pursuing enemy and allow themselves to break clean. Once into the wadi, they were able to fire and manoeuvre into better cover. The stranded Spartan now began to draw particular attention as the enemy realised that it was disabled. With 1 Platoon now visible the remainder of the Company Group's fire support weapons were now brought to bear, including artillery. This in turn caused the enemy to begin engaging the District Centre with RPG fire from within the town. In the wadi the HCR recovered the crew and specialist equipment from the Spartan, and all members of the Company Group

moved into positions to prevent the enemy from reaching the Spartan. This enabled one bomb to be dropped from Close Air Support which combined with heavy artillery and mortar fire forced the enemy to abandon the fight for the time being.

On 20th August, a patrol from 1 Platoon was moving north with two sections forward to provide protection to the third section that was using bar mines to create a covered route through a series of compounds. A WMIK (Land Rover) was with the forward left section, and a second WMIK supported by a fire team was deployed into the town covering approaches to the platoon's right flank. Cpl Bryan Budd was leading the forward right section, and as he moved forward he saw three enemy positions to his front which he indicated to his section organising them for attack. As he led them forward the WMIK on his left flank was ambushed, and there was an immediate requirement to regain the initiative. Budd pushed forward with the attack, entering a significant firefight. One member of the section was hit in the body armour, and LCpl Roberts, the Mortar Fire Controller attached to the platoon, was hit in the shoulder. As Pte Halton and Pte Lanaghan moved to pull LCpl Roberts into cover, Pte Lanaghan was hit in the face and arm. Pte Halton continued to extract LCpl Roberts and Pte Lanaghan while Cpl Budd continued the attack himself being wounded in the process. The section second in command pulled the section back to regroup unaware that Cpl Budd had been wounded as he moved forward. Cpl Budd was duly declared missing in action.

Cpl Bryan Budd VC who was killed at Sangin.

Private Briggs holds the bullet head that struck his body plate.

By this stage Lt Farmer and the third section had moved up. Lt Farmer led two attempts to move forward to where Cpl Budd was believed to have been, but both were driven back by enemy fire, wounding Cpl Curnow of 2 Section in the process. Pte Briggs, the radio operator was knocked to the ground with a round in his body armour, and Lt Farmer received a shrapnel wound to the buttocks. To the rear of the platoon the initial Quick Reaction Force was deployed forward to secure the casualty collection point. CSM Schofield made three trips with a quad bike and trailer to retrieve the casualties, himself coming under fire as he did so. A composite second platoon, under 2Lt Mallett, consisting of members of A Company, the Sniper Platoon, D Squadron HCR, 51 Para Sqn RE, and two members of the RMP (SIB) moved forward to reinforce 1 Platoon and try and approach Cpl Budd's position from a different direction. They too were pinned down by enemy fire. The enemy on the ground were now very close and trying to surround 1 Platoon's position.

Distances precluded the use of Close Air Support, and so Apaches were requested. The WMIK in the town covering the right flank identified enemy rushing weapons out of a mosque, and began to engage them with a mortar fire mission. Once the Apaches arrived, Lt Farmer was able to drive the enemy back, move forward and recover Cpl Budd. Sadly he was pronounced killed in action by the Regimental Medical Officer at the Regimental Aid Post. However, in the finest traditions of The Parachute Regiment, he would have taken enormous pride in the fact that when he was found his body was surrounded by three dead Taliban.

The intensity of enemy activity continued until 29th August when the remainder of the Battalion came to Sangin on Op BAGHI. This operation provided a ground resupply into the District Centre, inserted an air portable ferry bridge to open up an alternative logistic route across the river Helmand, and allowed C Company to conduct a Relief In Place (RIP) with A Company.

A Pathfinder pictured in action at Musa Qaleh.

The aftermath of a 500lb dropped near the town to silence a Taliban attack.

CHAPTERFIVE
→ THE FIGHT FOR MUSA QALEH

The Pathfinder Platoon was renamed Pathfinder Group during the deployment to Helmand.

A Pathfinder pictured at Musa Qaleh.

//THE FIGHT FOR MUSA QALEH
//THE PATHFINDERS

After their initial advance force operations and their spell at Musa Qaleh the Pathfinders (PF) returned to Forward Operating Base Price, where a number of operations were proposed and then cancelled. Finally, the Group were ordered to return to Musa Qaleh and relieve the US Army Unit who had previously replaced them. It is worth noting that the PF were just 24 strong and were sent in to relieve 150 Americans. Initially the OC was told that they would be in Musa Qaleh for between 48-96 hours. But due to drastic changes to the situation, the Group ended up staying in Musa Qaleh for 52 days, 26 of which were in direct contact with the enemy.

At the start of the deployment the situation was permissive. The Pathfinders conducted joint patrols with the Afghan Police and engaged with the tribal elders to ascertain their security aspirations. Concurrently the compound's defences were reinforced and built up as much as possible with local materials. Over this period intelligence indicated that the Taliban were closing in on Musa Qaleh; they viewed it as 'vital ground' to allow them to push their offensive south to Sangin. During this time the PF Group was reinforced by elements of 9 Para Squadron RE who were tasked to improve the Compound infrastructure – concentrating on security and sanitation. Reinforcements also came in the form of a troop from I Battery, 7 Para RHA, operating in the infantry role. Operations were conducted in the town – searches of suspect houses, Vehicle Check Points for drugs and normal framework patrols. Night time patrols were also conducted.

By the middle of July the Taliban started attacking the compound on a daily basis. These attacks ranged from stand-off small arms attacks and indirect fire, to co-ordinated full scale attacks from all directions. All units within the compound fought hard to keep the enemy out and inflicted casualties on the Taliban. At the beginning of this period the PF had artillery support from the Americans, then when they moved south air-power became the main support.

Over a ten day period the Group called in six artillery fire missions and 26 air strikes. On 26th July, the Danish Recce Squadron was able to breakthrough the Taliban lines and link-up with the British forces in Musa Qaleh; by this stage the force had been out of fresh water and rations for five days. Relying on water purification tablets and limited food purchased from the bazaar. The Engineers and Gunners were extracted the next day.

The Pathfinders remained in Musa Qaleh for another 10 days with the Danes. An escape attempt was attempted with the Danes on 1st August but the convoy was ambushed in a wadi and had to fight all the way back to the District Compound, miraculously this was achieved without injury. Five days later a Battle Group operation was conducted in the area and the Pathfinders were able to extract. With the Pathfinders back in FOB PRICE there was time to reconstitute, rehearse and plan the next operation which was to be a series of patrols into southern Helmand. The aim of these patrols was to bolster support for the local government and gain intelligence of the area. These patrols were all conducted in vehicles and re-supplied by air-drop and helicopter. Contact was had with the Taliban on two separate occasions. The first was during Op SARWE. The Pathfinder Group was tasked with securing a line of departure for a mixed force of OMLT, Afghan Army and Police to retake Garmser District Centre. On the way to securing the line they were engaged by accurate small arms and mortar fire. The enemy position was suppressed and the OMLT were able to move forward into their attack. The second contact happened as the Group returned to FOB Price. They were engaged at night by small arms fire.

These final patrols allowed the Group to hone its mobility skills and pushed men and machines to the limits of the endurance. Vehicles broke down on a daily basis and only good maintenance and support from the REME kept them operational.

The Pathfinders prepare to leave Musa Qaleh.

Danish troops under fire at Musa Qaleh.

A US Black Hawk airlifts a casualty out of Musa Qaleh.

//THE FIGHT FOR MUSA QALEH
//DANISH RECCE SQUADRON

The Danish Government had confirmed in 2005 that it intended to support the expansion of NATO forces into the south of the country in support of the Government of Afghanistan. The Ministry of Defence announced that it would deploy a Danish Reconnaissance Squadron and 'The Griffins Squadron' were sent to train with 3 PARA Battle Group in the UK and then deploy into Helmand Province. Well equipped with armoured vehicles and personal equipment the Danes soon found themselves in the thick of the action. In July they went into Musa Qaleh, alongside the Pathfinders and members of 3 PARA for what was to be a challenging experience.

Within their first couple of days at the DC in northern Helmand the Danes experienced heavy fighting. These are the words of one Danish solider: "There was a crack!. The bullet penetrating the sound barrier caught everyone by surprise. The next sound echoing off the walls in the Musa Qaleh District Centre (DC) was the shouting for a Medic …medic!… we need a medic on the outpost!" Whilst the rest of the platoon on guard opened fire on the Taliban sniper position north of the DC, Sgt Mathiesen was brought down from the sangar with a bullet through the back of his head. He was taken to the clinic in the southern end of the compound and an urgent transmission was made to Camp Bastion. Already overhead, RAF Harrier GR-7's instantly spotted three Taliban on motorcycles leaving the compound from which the sniper shot had come and followed their escape to the north. When they opened up again on us again and presented a threat we were able to engage them. This had been the beginning of yet another extremely busy day in Musa Qaleh for the Danish soldiers."

The Danish Squadron had arrived after five days in the desert which included a mine strike with three casualties and the destruction of a MOWAG Eagle armoured hummer. The Danes had been ambushed in the desert and had to use all sixteen of their .50 cal Heavy Macine Guns to fight off and destroy the Taliban, who had attacked on three sides simultaneously. The 84 mm Carl Gustav recoilless gun, a familiar weapon with the British Army in the 1970s, was used to deliver precise High Explosive airburst rounds over the enemy positions. Finally the Danes called in Close Air Support and a USAF B-1B bomber delivered a heavy blow to the Taliban.

Fast jet pilots and Apache crews became well aware of a Danish JTAC (Joint Tactical Air Controller) whose callsign must remain anonymous. His accuracy in target recognition became well known by the air crews and he achieved great success. What is less well know is that he was almost killed in a Taliban attack. During a attack on the Musa Qaleh DC his sangar was hit by a RPG round, with the resulting effect that the sangar collapsed. He fell from the second floor to street level injuring his leg and head.

The wall of the building facing the street also collapsed and the Dane was sitting with only his 9mm pistol as he waited for the enemy to move forward and kill him. Covering the rescue mission to get him out of the hole, a Danish colleague, Cpl George, put down accurate suppressive fire on the advancing enemy fighters and killed three before they could reach the hole in the wall. Then thanks to members of the Pathfinders who supported the Danes he was rescued and flown out.

When the Danes had entered Musa Qaleh to join the Pathfinders all they saw was dirty, skinny, heavily armed and bearded British soldiers. All of them smiling like 7-year-old schoolboys on Christmas morning, so happy were they to see reinforcements. On that first day the Taliban attacked the base and had something of a surprise when the significant increase in force numbers returned fire with sixteen .50 cal HMG, ten GPMG's and nine 84 mm Carl Gustavs. Some of the Taliban attacks were chilling as they simply ran shooting at the DC under heavy and accurate sustained fire! Over a 33 day period the Danes had 60 incidents, some close quarter and other stand off attacks in which rockets were fired. Such was the intensity of the fighting that on many occasions CAS was called in with support from French Mirages, Dutch F-16s, US F-18Fs, US Harriers, B-1B Bombers, A-10s, RAF GR7s and of course the Apaches.

A Company found themselves engaged in a major firefight.

The company was flown in by Chinooks with Apache escorts.

//THE FIGHT FOR MUSA QALEH
//US CONVOY ATTACKED

On 13th June 2006 A Company Group was in Camp Bastion preparing for an operation when news came in that an American logistics convoy had been ambushed and was in need of assistance. The convoy had suffered one killed in action and one wounded in action, and were dismounted in a hasty defence around their vehicles, fending off repeated Taliban attacks and unable to move. With briefings complete the Company Group headed north to the ambush site between Sangin and Musa Qala. Having located the ambush site, the Chinooks landed in a large open space under the protection of three Apaches. Almost immediately the Taliban fired an RPG at one of the helicopters, exploding just underneath it, and setting the tone for what was to come.

The convoy had stopped near some high ground that offered itself as a good defensive position. With light fading rapidly the Company began to establish a hasty defensive position, helping the Americans to salvage key equipment from their damaged vehicles and to recover one of their low loaders. Undamaged vehicles were moved into some dead ground for protection, and four man shell scrapes were quickly dug and occupied. The plan was to defend this position until first light before moving further into the desert to rendezvous with and hand over responsibility to an American unit.

Shortly before 2100 hrs the Taliban returned and engaged the defensive position with a heavy weight of fire coordinated from a number of positions. The enemy used AK variants, RPGs and most notably a heavy machine gun firing from the cover of a nearby village. The rounds were accurate and the hastily dug shallow shell scrapes prevented the Company from taking a number of casualties. It was A Company's first night contact and being clearly able to see the path of the bullets gave the experience a new, more sinister character.

Initially A Company was pinned down by the weight of fire but as Taliban positions were identified the Company were able to engage them, subduing the enemy until the attack faltered and stopped. A Company Group were unhurt, but its US colleagues had sustained two casualties after a direct RPG hit on one of the Humvees. One casualty had a significant shrapnel wound to the neck which thankfully had been cauterized in the explosion of the RPG, but the other casualty was in a serious condition. He had suffered a significant head wound that had taken the top of his skull off, causing the loss of one eye, and additionally had several bullet wounds to the arms and legs.

Both casualties were stabilised by Pte McKinley from 1 Platoon and LCpl Roberts, the medic, attached to the Company. A request for casevac was submitted, however the enemy were not yet finished, and keen for another go, and began to prepare for another attack. But Cpl Wright's section spotted a group of enemy forming up, and pre-empted them inflicting many casualties on the Taliban. Cpl Mark Wright, the Mortar Fire Controller, then called in 35 rounds of 81mm High Explosive (HE) onto a compound that the enemy were using as a second position to form up, destroying it and a number of insurgents in the process.

With their second attack failing to even get started the enemy then withdrew. The rest of the night was quiet as the enemy licked their wounds. The Chinook arrived to casevac the two casualties who both lived thanks largely to the efforts made by 3 PARA soldiers. At first light the Company withdrew into the desert and waited for the US link up. Low on food and water, an emergency resupply was called in. Fourteen hours later the Company handed over to a huge US convoy and flew back to the quiet comfort of Camp Bastion.

Paratroopers ay their way towards the Chinooks for passage back to Bastion.

81

RAF Chinooks low and fast as they make their exit from Musa Qaleh.

A Royal Irish Ranger in the streets of Musa Qaleh.

82

//THE FIGHT FOR MUSA QALEH

//THE ROYAL IRISH REGIMENT

The Royal Irish Regiment was warned off in July 2006 to provide two rifle platoons and a mortar section, at short notice to reinforce 3 PARA Battle Group in southern Afghanistan, as part of Operation HERRICK. This was in addition to Ranger Platoon who had already joined the Battle Group in April. This brought the 1 R IRISH commitment to 3 PARA Battle Group to 98 soldiers. The Commanding Officer of 1 R IRISH tasked D Company and B Company to form a rifle platoon each. As a result, the company commanders were overwhelmed by eager volunteers from across the battalion who were keen to deploy to Afghanistan for a slice of the action. Once Barossa Platoon was formed by B Company and Somme Platoon by D Company, a busy training period followed to prepare the two platoons and the Mortar Section. As those selected to deploy prepared to leave Fort George the Commanding Officer gave them a final brief in which he warned that the tour would be hectic and that the Taliban was a formidable enemy. His comments were right on all counts. The journey into Afghanistan and on to Camp Bastion went well and on arrival the R IRISH were attached to D 'Gurkha' Company to assist with the security of Bastion which also gave time to acclimatise. Despite the fact that the Gurkhas were excellent hosts the platoons had not wanted to get hooked up in camp security for too long and were desperate to get on the ground.

After just four days in Helmand, Somme Platoon and the Mortar Section were warned off for operations. They were to reinforce the in-place Danish Recce Squadron at the District Centre in Musa Qaleh and allow the Pathfinders to be extracted. Many of the R IRISH soldiers will remember the smiling faces of the Pathfinders, who waved on their way out and viewed Musa Qaleh in their rear view mirrors. At Musa Qaleh the R IRISH were placed under the command of the Danish Recce Squadron which provided a fourth manoeuvre element to the force. The Mortar Section quickly began adjusting a defensive fire plan and shortly after the first attack came.

One soldier recalled: "Within minutes of arriving we received the local welcome, and experienced our first of many attacks to come. Our initial impression of the town itself was surreal; it was an absolute ghost town, all civilians had fled a few days before our arrival as the fighting intensified in the town. It was just the Taliban on the outside, and 38 Irishmen and 140 Danish Vikings on the inside. Our first impressions of the Danish were that they were superbly equipped and well organised. They had more vehicles, mounted machine guns, heavy machine guns and recoilless rifles than you could shake a stick at. They also had a mobile industrial fridge and water purifier. The Danish rations were also far tastier than ours and we quickly struck up an excellent rapport with our new hosts."

Before the Irish troops had arrived the Danes had suffered a number of casualties from well coordinated ground attacks, and on the third day in Musa Qaleh two soldiers from Somme Platoon were airlifted out of the base with gunshot wounds. This incident quickly focussed the force and demonstarted the capability of the enemy. The frequency of the Taliban attacks was relentless for those inside Musa Qaleh. The contacts, otherwise know as TICs (Troops in Contact),were recorded almost everyday at the District Centre as MQ became a hotbed for insurgent activity. The Taliban were well equipped with small arms, RPGs, Chinese rockets, recoilless rifles and mortars.

On 24th August the Danish Squadron extracted and was replaced by an additional 1 R IRISH platoon (Barossa) and a Company Headquarter element from 3 PARA. It was just what Musa Qaleh needed, another 28 mad Irishmen. As a result of the combined Parachute Regiment and R IRISH contingent 'Easy' Company 3 PARA was formed, with 90% wearing the Green Hackle and Shamrock. Naturally enough, the Taliban had thought that the Coalition resolve had been broken when they saw the large Danish convoy extracting from the district compound. They were clearly under the impression that the compound had been abandoned and left to be defended by just the Afghan National Police, providing the opportunity for them to launch a major assault and over run the base.

In a matter of hours after the Danes had left the Taliban attacked with a combination of small arms fire, RPG, AGS 17 (Grenade Launcher), 107mm Rocket and 82mm Mortar, they were organised and co-ordinated. The Company defeated the assault and more followed. The fighting in the following weeks was ferocious and at close quarters, with grenades thrown over the walls and fast jet fire power regularly called as close as 30 metres away from the DC. The Company had increasing volumes of fixed wing aircraft pushed its way during the fighting with support from F 16, F 18, B1 Bombers and RAF Harriers. In one month the UK Harrier force based in Kandahar flew a hundred missions in support of the Company. On one memorable day an RAF Harrier was directed towards an enemy gun team near the DC, the pilot responded to the JTAC on the ground: 'I see your carnage' as he viewed the sparse remains of the Musa Qaleh DC, which suffered many attacks.

The Company had eight light role GPMG and a pair of HMG that were mounted in open sangars on the key buildings. Over a quarter of all 7.62mm link fired on Op HERRICK in 2006 was used by Easy Company fighting in Musa Qaleh as were a fifth of the Grenades. Due to the intensity of the fighting and the fact the Company was frequently in combat over the Helicopter Landing Site, Support Helicopters could not be flown in following two "Cherry" (Hot LS) calls in early September.

83

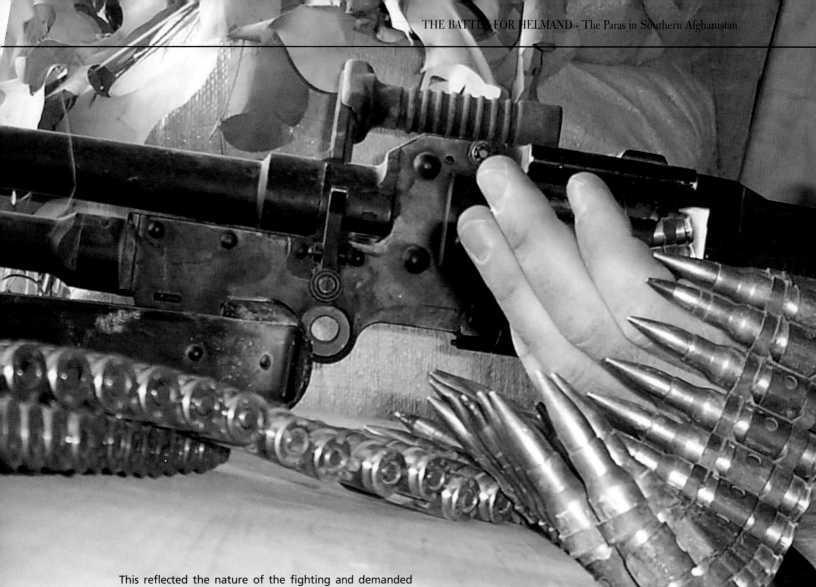

This reflected the nature of the fighting and demanded more innovation from the Company in its modus operandi. The last CASEVAC flight fortunately brought in a complete Battlefield Casualty Replacement Section and Platoon Commander from B Coy 3 PARA (Additional to three KIA, 12 of the Company had to be CASEVACed, evacuated out by helicopter). Dummy guns were made after one of the HMG was destroyed on the "Alamo" position and the failing infrastructure was managed through sheer determination as generators were super glued together to keep drawing water from the well. Throughout their stay in Musa Qaleh, the Company had outstanding support form the Scimitars of the HCR and 7 Para RHA who provided support from remote desert locations.

In September the company suffered a major setback when two soldiers from Somme, LCpl Muirhead and Ranger Draiva, were killed, and another 12 soldiers from Somme and Barossa were wounded in action. During one particular engagement, Lt Martin, Barossa Platoon, and six men from one section were wounded.

Lt Martin and the others were airlifted back to the UK and replaced by men from 3 PARA, flown in as Battlefield Casualty Replacements. One Afghan policeman was also killed and five were also wounded in action.

Supply to the compound was limited, and only came when casualties were flown out. When the aircraft were being prepared at Bastion, ground crews would pack them with food, water and ammunition as well as any urgent equipment requirements. In the main those in Musa Qaleh ate ration pack food and drank water from a well. The Company saw Musa Qaleh through an intense period of fighting and into an enduring time of peace, established at the end of our tour. That peace came with a cost, three of the Company died in the fighting: LCpl Hetherington, Rgr Draiva and LCpl Muirhead.

Manning the General Purpose Machine Gun at Musa Qaleh.

Soldiers remember fallen comrades at the Memorial Cairn in Bastion.

Rangers advance towards Musa Qaleh and right, a R IRISH mortar team prepares the 81mm inside the DC.

Bayonets fixed, Paratroopers are briefed before an operation.

//THE FIGHT FOR MUSA QALEH

//THE TOWN OF MUSA QALEH

Musa Qaleh is situated in the north of the Area of Operation. It appears at first glance to be a quiet market town. It is obviously tribal and, like the entire region limited in its infrastructure and resources with the main economy based around local trading stalls. But behind the smiles of local people and the waving hands of the children the Taliban had held the town in a vice like grip for many years. Situated north of Sangin, the town Musa Qaleh commands the gateway to Sangin, the main collection and distribution point for the opium trade. Some of the Taliban's key figures had, it was claimed, been hiding out in Musa Qaleh and regarded the town as theirs before British forces arrived. Prior to 2006, the Taliban had regularly attacked US forces in the area and claimed on the internet to have a force of 200 fighters in the town. The Pathfinders were the first Brits into the town during preliminary operations and their assessment was that Musa Qaleh had the potential to be a major headache in respect of the overall plan to deliver security and start the planned phase of reconstruction. Fighting had started in Musa Qaleh after the Taliban attacked the District Centre and British troops moved in to reinforce Afghan police and prevent the base being overrun. By mid summer 2006 the offensive action around the DC was intense with Taliban in-direct attacks sometimes missing the DC and causing death and destruction among the local population. In a bid to stop the bloodshed and allow the people of Musa Qaleh to take the initiative, Brigadier Ed Butler headed a Shura at which it was proposed that the village elders take charge. After extensive talks a 'cessation of violence' was agreed in which the village elders ordered the Taliban out of the town. The ceasefire saw the return of peace and daily life in Musa Qaleh for several months.

A sniper team pictured in Sangin at the height of the deployment.

Paratroopers pause for thought at the end of an operation.

CHAPTERSIX
→ PERSONAL ACCOUNTS

89

LCpl Jeff Thomas pictured at Now Zad after a series of firefights with the Taliban.

//PERSONAL ACCOUNTS
//A SOLDIER'S STORY

LCpl Jeff Thomas of B Company, 3 PARA, was part of a ten Land Rover (WMIKs) convoy that deployed in support of A Company at Now Zad. Their task was to create a cordon around the compound to prevent Taliban escaping while A Company were in the town flushing the enemy out. As the vehicles headed down a narrow road, they had a ditch to the right and a wall to the left. Sudenly as the vehicles turned left, the lead vehicle was confronted by a compound full of Taliban. They were immediately engaged with small arms fire and rocket propelled grenades as the lead vehicle, reversed as quickly as it could out of the compound whilst returning fire with .50 cal, GPMG and SA80 fire. The second vehicle saw the enemy and also reversed. As they sped backwards several Land Rovers hit each other, but were able to quickly cover ground to a safe location where they could re-group.

LCpl Thomas, aged 21, recalls: "We were left with only one option, that was to press on forward. We had a treeline to our left and a large ditch to the right, if we'd gone back we would have gone straight back into the compound we'd just left, so forward was the only feasible option "As they proceeded they were ambushed from the treeline by a number of Taliban. He added: "They were firing at quite a rate, Small Arms and RPG were coming our way. The 'top cover' – .50 calibre – was quick to engage, showering the tree line with rounds"

The convoy continued to engage the Taliban for approximately 15 minutes of constant fire. Thomas adds: "After about 15 minutes of hitting them (the Taliban) with a lot of fire power the attack ceased, it was our opportunity to press on and take up our positions on the outskirts of the town".

The convoy moved on, with the top cover and everyone else carefully scanning the tree line for more enemy movement. LCpl Thomas and his colleagues had still not finished fighting the enemy. He said: "A Company went into the town between 1100 hrs and 1200 hrs, the intention was to capture some key Taliban figures, we were there to prevent them running off. The convoy was then involved in another contact which lasted two hours as the enemy attacked them from three different compounds."

LCpl Thomans concluded: "We wanted to press forward and engage the Taliban that were ahead firing on us. But we couldn't risk the possibility of firing on A company. The convoy was on task until A company were lifted out of Now Zad. Unofficial figures suggest between 18 and 22 Taliban were killed by our convoy alone. Between us we fired in excess of 4000 rounds". By the time the convoy had been extracted it had been on the ground for seven hours.

[*Top cover - Military term for the gunner in the back of the Land Rover who stands up and looks out, providing 'top cover'*]

The Band of Brothers from 4 and 5 Platoons.

The open terrain around Sangin.

//PERSONAL ACCOUNTS
//BAND OF BROTHERS

The paratroopers of 4 and 5 Platoons of 3 PARA found themselves supporting operations across Helmand throughout their tour. Early August 2006 found them back in Sangin District Centre, where they were to be based for more than four weeks. No day was alike, yet every day was similar. They were under constant attack from Rocket Propelled Grenades, Small Arms Fire, concentrated machine gun fire and mortars. These young paratroopers were manning sangars (lookout posts) around the clock and were on constant alert, even in their down time, for an incoming attack.

On the 29th August, B Company were involved in what the military term a 'deliberate operation' (a planned and prepared mission), called Op BAGHI. The aim of the operation was to mount a cordon of protection to allow a re-supply of Sangin to take place and provide cover for the Royal Engineers who were to build and install a ferry bridge across the River Helmand. The bridge was important as it would provide a second route into the District Centre for men and vehicles and in the longer term would possibly be used by the public. The bridge was to be delivered by a huge convoy of trucks and would take a day to erect.

LCpl Paul Gordon, aged 25, remembers the mission well. He said: "We were briefed on the operation, and given instructions on our specific objective. B Company was to secure the north and C Company was to secure the south. Our aim was to get to a location we termed the Chinese Restaurant which was about 700 metres from the District Centre and provide perimeter security for the re-supply and the engineers as they erected the ferry bridge."

At 0700 hrs the following morning, when it was still cool, the troops left Sangin District Centre. Wearing 50lbs of essential kit, which included anti tank missiles, grenades, ammunition and water, as well as in some cases ladders to assault buildings. These paratroopers needed to be fit. They carefully made their way, aware that the Taliban were likely to be in the area. But before they had even covered 100 metres they were attacked.

Ian Potter, a 23-year-old paratrooper said: "For 15 minutes we took constant incoming and accurate heavy machine gun and RPG fire. We were pinned down in the location for what seemed ages."

Having assessed that there were between three and five Taliban approximately 300 metres ahead, suppressing their position, the need to push forward and get away from where they were stuck was imperative for the Paras and they quickly advanced forward using the side streets as cover. Paratrooper Joe Richardson, aged 18, said: "We'd made it to pretty much the half way point. From our position we could see that the Taliban that were firing at us were hiding in the Chinese Restaurant, where we were heading."

The enemy fire had by now increased, but in order to move forward and be ready for the main phase of the operation now faced a 200-metre dash across open ground. The firing from the Chinese Restaurant was now even heavier, as the Paras waited to make their move. Paratrooper Matthew Broomhead, aged 19, said: "We were waiting for the signal to start the forward push."

Paratrooper Ian Potter pictured during the operation.

A brief moment to capture history: Second Lieutenant Ollie Dale, who won the MC, and men of 8 Platoon pose for a photo after a long operation.

The signal was to be a JDAM bombing run from an RAF Harrier – on the restaurant. (A JDAM is a Joint Direct Attack Munition – a target directed and very accurate bomb.)

Paratrooper Nathan Pleace recalls: "As we were waiting for the JDAM our company commander gave us a bit of a talk to boost our confidence. He told us 'maximum speed and aggression lads, this is why you joined the army. It's not gonna get anymore real than this' - and he was right." Shortly afterwards the aircraft could be heard overhead. Paratrooper Charles Suku, 22, said: "The JDAM struck, right on target. It was an awesome sight as the Harrier flew over and dropped the bomb, next thing the target pretty much exploded."

The troop barely had time to take in the sight, the bombing run had been their signal to advance, and after the confusion created they weren't about to waste the opportunity. Individually, but at a pace they crossed the 200 metres of open ground. They made it to their objective, and took cover in what was left of the Chinese Restaurant. The lads of 4 and 5 Platoon who were about 100 metres apart had a short respite, but then the Taliban realised what was going on and the firing started.

Paratrooper Dennis O'Kane said: "About five minutes after we'd settled in the firing started again. We were taking incoming fire from machine guns and RPGs, from pretty much all directions, we felt almost like sitting ducks because we had to hold our position, again our training kicked in and we engaged the enemy firing positions."

The Taliban appeared to be in significant numbers and as well as being well armed they were hiding among the local community. An enemy mortar base plate or a large number of enemy that posed a threat to the operation could be engaged by air and ground forces but not when civilians were in danger.

LCpl Gordon said: "From our positions we could see that the Taliban were taking casualties. They were getting themselves into a building and attacking us harder, but we couldn't call for an air strike as they were taking women and children in with them. In some cases they were using the local population as human shields, it was sick, but we couldn't engage them for fear of hitting innocent civilians."

The aim of the operation was going successfully, the re-supply convoy had made it through and the ferry bridge was being installed at a fast rate. The lads of 4 Troop had been on the ground for over eight hours and had been under almost constant attack. They had conserved ammunition where possible, but had still fired more than 200 rounds each. At 1700 hrs they received the order to extract back to Sangin District Centre, they passed the message to 5 Platoon and started to peel back. During their extraction the mortar platoon provided covering fire throughout.

Paratrooper Ian Potter added: "The mortars were landing about 200 metres ahead of our position. As we pulled back the mortars pulled back with us staying at the same distance all the way."

Matthew Broomhead added: "The Taliban were aware of what was going on and intensified their rate of fire. They even tried to use motorbikes against us in order to break through the mortars, but we continued to return fire and they didn't succeed." At around 1800 hrs the two Platoons made it back into the District Centre. Joe Richardson added: "We were low on water and ammo but high on morale. Although we'd taken some casualties the operation had been a success and we were proud of what we'd achieved."

Back in the limited safety of Sangin, paratroopers reflect on their experiences.

//PERSONAL ACCOUNTS
//SIGNALLERS' STORIES

Corporal Woodward of 216 Signal Squdron, was assigned to 3 PARA and was based at Camp Bastion Rear Link Detachment. (A term used in respect of maintaining communications across the BG). He said: "It was a Friday morning in Bastion and I had just been told the bad news that I was going to remain in Bastion for a month. Then a stroke of luck and news came through that I was to deploy with 10 Platoon, Royal Gurkha Regiment to Now Zad as the Rear Link Detachment. I was off to replace Cpl Steel who had been with B Company 3 PARA along with LCpl Cook and LCpl Armstrong. The action came very fast as A Company mounted a deliberate operation into the town. For me it was an amazing experience. Things soon calmed down for a few weeks and we managed to get into a bit of a routine. This meant an opportunity to enjoy some delicious Gurkha goat curries. After a few weeks LCpl Cook and LCpl "Stretch" Armstrong were relieved by LCpl Rankin and Sig Whiltshire. Then a week later it was my turn to be relieved and back to Gereshk I went. It was an experience of a life time, both working with the Gurkhas, enjoying their friendship and curries and most of all doing the job for real!"

Signaller Barrett of 216 Signal Squdron, was attached to the Pathfinder Platoon Rear Link Detachment (PF RLD) He said: "The PF RLD left 216 a month before we were due to deploy in order integrate with the Pathfinder lads as well as get all the equipment ready. We were kept busy with build up training prior to the operation including comms, medical and deployment training. We deployed on a two week exercise and ran through scenarios we would most likely encounter in Afghanistan. PF RLD deployed to Afghanistan with the Pathfinder Platoon on 10th March. The Detachment started with an intense training package in Kandahar including range packages with the PF's weapon systems, which included GPMG, Minimi and the 51 mm Mortar.

"We got stuck into learning Standard Operating Procedures, and got introduced to the new comms systems that we would be using for the duration of the tour. Sgt "Chin" Clayton assisted with these lessons, as he was already familiar with these systems. The learning curve was steep as it was our first tour for the majority us. The shift pattern was quite exhausting with only two people, doing the lovely 12 hours on 12 hours off. I moved to Gereshk for three months after R&R in the UK, probably the best experience of my life! COP Price is a small but well constructed camp, with a gym and well air-conditioned. It was an amazing experience."

Lance Corporal "Flames" Sloan of 216 Signal Squdron, was attached to the Danish Rear Link Detachment at Musa Qaleh. He said: "On 21st of August myself and Signaller "Rooney" Griffiths set out from Camp Bastion as part of the Danish 1st Recce Sqn bound for the district centre of Musa Qaleh. We were deployed as a Relief in Place for the UK Pathfinder Platoon. Our job was to provide the Danes with a Tactical Satellite link back to HQ Helmand Task Force at Kandahar as well as providing a ground to air link for the Danish JTACs. It was no surprise when we were told that a group of 30 Taliban were planning to ambush us on route, lucky for us they weren't aware that we knew and we managed to avoid the ambush, the JTAC managing to call in Close Air Support. When we finally arrived at the outskirts of Musa Qaleh there was yet another ambush waiting for us, we were engaged with Heavy Machine Gun fire, RPG and to top it off the Taliban had blocked the road with barrels. We then moved into the desert and after five days we pushed back into town and into the Platoon House. We were attacked daily with everything in the Taliban arsenal from RPG, Chinese rockets, snipers, mortars, heavy machine gun fire, small arms and their favourite and probably the worst, the recoilless rifle. This piece of kit makes an awesome noise when it's incoming. The patrol house itself was made up of mud and steel girders. There were some very nice afghan rugs on the floor inside however these were full of fleas and where promptly burnt. The Danes were a top bunch of blokes and shared a similar sense of humour to our own, which made the days go a lot quicker as we taught them the art of exchanging banter."

Captain Ian Flannery of 216 Signal Squdron - served with the Operational Mentoring and Liaison Team at Camp Tombstone. He recalls "I deployed to Camp TOMBSTONE as part of the advance party to set up and establish a communications infrastructure for our team of 90 mentors.

"Taking over from a small group of US reservists, we were to train and mentor 3 Brigade of the Afghan National Army's 205 Corps. We arrived as the first Kandak (an Afghan Army battalion) had graduated from training and began the first cycle of training with them as soon as we hit the ground. The small 216 team set to work immediately on improving their already impressive communications. I was responsible for mentoring Maj (Jagman) Rahmanullah, who was quickly identified as the most switched on of the Afghan staff officers. As the tour progressed we became a little stretched, with another three Kandaks arriving during the tour and mobilisations to populate out-stations and undertake operations in the thick of the action. Though I was fairly well anchored to the Bde HQ, I did make it up to Sangin for a few weeks, to gain a better view of how communications were working on the ground and managed to get involved in the first big contact of the operation. Our patrol did well to survive a full on Taliban ambush with only one priority 1 casualty, LBdr Mason of 7 Para RHA, who made a full recovery. The QRF were not as lucky and lost Capt Jim Philippson, also of 7 Para RHA, when they were ambushed on their way to aid us. The accompanying 216 RLD got involved with low level comms mentoring and were all deployed to the out-stations for varying periods, Cpl Corbett was particularly active and saw action in most locations. In all, a highly successful tour, leaving the Afghan National Army in far better condition than we found it."

//PERSONAL ACCOUNTS
//THE PATROLS PLATOON

A paratrooper from the Patrols Platoon recounts his experience on one of the initial operations in Now Zad. He said: "On the 4th June, we took part in Operation MUTAY in Now Zad. We didn't really know what to expect, but when the firing started it was clear it was them or us and we malleted them, but it wasn't easy, some of them seemed to have no concern for their own life and attacked in full frontal fashion.

"As we attempted to establish screening positions to the west of A Company's cordon and search, we came under fire from the enemy in three separate incidents. The first was during the move into position, when we were the lead callsign (the front Land Rover) and ran into a group of heavily armed Taliban. We returned fire and it seemd to end as quickly as it had started and although we had no casualties, many of us felt we had been lucky. The opening barrage from the enemy had included a RPG (Rocket Proplled Grenade) which had knocked a branch from a tree directly above the Platoon's Pinzgauer vehicle which was carrying signallers and the Platoon's Air Controller.

"After a short period to re-balance and receive direction from higher command, we moved off to attempt to establish alternative screen positions to the west of A Company's ongoing operation (which itself was being hampered by numerous firefights with enemy forces). As we moved carefully along a track, which was very difficult as the vehicles were restricted by the walls and irrigation ditches on either side, a small enemy force ambushed the convoy again.

Smoke grenade on a soldier's webbing.

"Contact was close and sudden. We had clearly sprung an ill-prepared and undermanned ambush, and we quickly suppressed the enemy with an accurate weight of fire before moving onto an area of cover for the vehicles. At this point, and after having had another RPG fired at one of the vehilces from close range, there was concern that a vehicle would be lost to a RPG strike if the Platoon continued to operate mounted in this area.

"The decision was therefore made to extract the vehicles into open ground where their weapon systems could be employed to greater effect before returning to the area with as many dismounted soldiers as possible in order to close with the enemy. However, before this plan could be executed a group of Taliban was seen moving to reinforce the ambush by a member of the Platoon who subsequently engaged them. The firefight became heavy as the Platoon found itself desperately attempting to protect the vehicles, and we exchanged fire for some time.

"Our fire control orders and general fire discipline again proved instrumental. The more accurate weight of fire suppressed the enemy long enough to extract the vehicles while a number of dismounts attempted to clear the compound in which the last group of enemy had been seen to enter. Blood trails and signs of a struggled withdrawal were found and followed up, but no further enemy were seen.

"During the third contact, one of the drivers was hit by 7.62mm rounds that ricocheted off the magazines in his chest rig, igniting the tracer rounds it contained. While in contact, a HMG gunner was knocked out of his WMIK (Land Rover) after receiving a round direct into the sternum plate of his Osprey body armour. Having regained his bearings, he re-mounted the vehicle and continued to engage the enemy. Despite these events, the enemy fire was heavy but not accurate. One enemy RPG gunner was so successfully suppressed that he was forced to fire his weapon from around a corner without using the sights before being neutralised. Everyone from the Platoon felt lucky to have escaped without having sustained casualties. All were surprised by the tenacity of the enemy who continued the fight despite being enormously overmatched both from the ground and the air.

"The Air Controller had successfully called for fire from a supporting Apache that had in turn engaged and suppressed a number of targets in depth as well as in close proximity to 3 PARA personnel. The soldiers developed respect for the Taliban who continued the battle until they were engaged at close range by HMG (Heavy Machine Gun) and GPMG (General Purpose Machine Gun)."

//PERSONAL ACCOUNTS
//THE LOGISTICS STORY

2Lt Hannah Bedford of the RLC recalls her experience on Operation BAGHI, the mission to build a ferry bridge at Sangin. She said: "Operation BAGHI was a deliberate operation to re-supply and deliver bridging equipment to the Sangin District Centre (DC) compound, home to A Company of 3 PARA and several small detachments of other units. The building of a bridge would enable the DC to be accessed via two routes rather than one and reduce risk to any future re-supply operation. A number of units were involved including 51 Para Squadron Royal Engineers, Joint Force EOD, I Battery 7 Para RHA and the Afghan National Army with The Household Cavalry Regt (HCR) and Royal Gurkha Rifles (RGR) providing protection for us.

"It was an early start on Monday 28th August. We left Camp Bastion in a twenty-five vehicle convoy bound for Combat Outpost Post (COP) Robinson, an operating base to the south of Sangin. It was approximately an hour before we reached Route One, the only main road through Afghanistan. We travelled through Gereshk with overhead support of Apache attack helicopters to deter the Taliban, before turning north through the desert. The terrain was tough for all the drivers with a mixture of deep sand, rocky patches, flat plains and mountainous areas. After twelve long hours of driving and struggling to pick out features and paths that were marked on maps but not visible on the ground, the Force Protection Troop (RLC soldiers) led us safely to COP ROBINSON.

"We were ready very early, the following morning in our vehicles waiting for 3 PARA to secure the town and call us forward and after a delay we finally left the camp at 0730 hrs. Seven kilometers north of ROBINSON, we drove into the desert and the wadi in which we would be crossing to enter the town. This was a crucial task as it was the only route into the DC and the open ground was subject to enemy attack. In addition the risk of IEDs (Improvised Explosive Devices) and mines being laid was high and it was difficult to keep our presence secret. After all we were a two kilometre long convoy.

"As we entered the wadi, everyone was on alert scouring the ground in front of us as well as looking for figures on either side of the bank. Sangin has not been particularly welcoming for UK forces and we were expecting the worst. As we came into the town, it was deserted, eerily quiet and quite surreal. Anyone with any sense had left, knowing what might happen. Despite feeling it, we weren't alone, there were Paras covering us from several buildings and positions. We observed their heads poking over rooftops. Seeing the DC compound within metres was a welcome sight and we sped into it.

"Within minutes of our arrival, our peace was shattered by the sound of incoming mortars and small arms fire. The Paras' response was the impressive sound of a .50 calibre machine gun returning fire from a tower above us. The OC ran over and informed me that we were going to move out of the DC at best speed to give the Taliban the minimum amount of time to reinforce their position before our exit. We were given the time limit of one hour to complete the offload. Having briefed the soldiers and liaised with camp personnel as to the positioning of kit, the speed at which the soldiers got to work was impressive.

"Despite several interruption calls of 'Take Cover!' from 3 PARA's RSM, the camp was a hive of activity. Being inside the DC did not give us a warm fuzzy feeling because there were certain areas where the Taliban could shoot at us. I thought a Staff Sergeant from the Engineers was joking when he shouted 'Right ma'am, are you ready to sprint as fast as you can across this bridge? They will shoot down the stream!' but more incoming fire assured me he was not joking. We were practiced at securing CVRT(Scimitars) on flat racks and loaded and secured one in a record time of fifteen minutes: practice makes perfect. Several hundred litres of sweat were shed in those sixty minutes, all the while wearing the heavy and uncomfortable Osprey body armour and helmets.

"Once everything was done we were sat in our vehicles waiting for the call to go. Everyone was keen to get out of Sangin, but not quite so keen to see what was going to happen on our way out. The soldiers were all very quiet as we were all contemplating the minutes ahead of us. As we pulled out of the gate we were looking around waiting for something to happen. A few minutes passed and we were back out into the wadi. Once in relative safety we stopped to ensure everybody was present and to re-adjust any loose loads that had been done in haste. It was now mid-afternoon and we headed back to COP ROBINSON. The cross-country move there was slow due to our loads. After a few problems, we made it to the camp as the sun was disappearing over the horizon.

"Again we were up early and moving out for our final part of the operation. The journey back was a struggle for the tired drivers and commanders but everyone drove well and we made impressive time. As we turned south off the MSR, Camp Bastion came into view and smiles began to appear on the tired faces! The operation was a success and most importantly we came back with all personnel and vehicles."

The morale of paratroopers was high from the day of their arrival.

In a lighter moment during the operation, C Company organised a moustache growing competition. Here the 21C, CSM and OC (Major Paddy Blair) warm up prior to the judging.

//PERSONAL ACCOUNTS
//THE PARAS' FIGHTING SPIRIT

The spirit of 3 PARA Battle Group is summed LCpl Danny Kelly, 21, of B Company. He said: "Bravo Company spent about a month in Sangin. We were living in the District Centre and we were getting about three or four contacts a day. One of my lasting memories will be the 6th July, we hadn't been there long and it was my 21st birthday. Many of my mates were laughing and joking about it, saying 'cracking birthday mate' and generally trying to cheer me up with their black humour. But for me not many people can say that they were shot at, mortared and had RPGs flying metres over their head on their 21st. It's a birthday I'll never forget. Overall I'd sum up my time in Afghanistan as; tough at times, hard at times, sad at times and very good at times. But we're paratroopers and we are always gonna work to the max. I think the lads have been excellent, we've worked our socks off and have done The Parachute Regiment proud."

Pte Shaun Robb served with B Company across Helmand at Now Zad, Musa Qaleh, Kajaki and of course Sangin. His story highlights the pride that all paratroopers took with them into southern Afghanistan and reinforces the value of training undertaken by soldiers of The Parachute Regiment. Pte Robb is extremely proud of what he and his fellow paras achieved in Helmand. He said "We were given a months acclimatisation training before deploying which prepared us for the job in hand. We arrived expecting to go in guns blazing, but we quickly realised that we were the, stronger, better equipped and more prepared force.

"I will personally never forget Sangin, definitely Sangin Valley. We – B Company 3 PARA – were deployed in the District Centre for about a month and while we were there we came under contact everyday. It was hot and dusty, but we had lots of food and water. Morale remained high because we were doing what we were trained to do, I think we would have been more disappointed if we hadn't had any contact with the Taliban." On one occasion in mid August elements of both Bravo and Charlie companies were deployed in Sangin. They were preparing for a resupply of the District Centre and were to secure the perimeter to the North of the town. Pte Robb's company was to advance northwest and secure the perimeter so that the resupply convoy could get through. At 0600, Bravo company deployed from Sangin. Their task was to cover just over a kilometre of varying terrain to the edge of the town, dig in and wait for the convoy to pass.

As was so common at Sangin, the company had barely made it 100 metres when they were suddenly under enemy fire. Small arms fire was coming at them from ahead. "We weren't expecting contact so early on but we were prepared. Our training kicked in and we responded by getting some rounds down quickly. We formed a baseline and pushed forward onto the enemy position clearing the compound and killing the Taliban." Said Pte Robb.

Once within the compound the company had a chance to regroup and take stock before they pressed on. At 0700 hrs they moved out of the compound, the objective still had to be achieved, the perimeter security was paramount. This time they progressed a little over 50 metres before they were under contact again. It was a familiar drill; baseline, push forward, suppress the enemy, regroup and move on. Twice more they came into contact before reaching their position approximately one kilometre away. It had taken them a good two hours to reach their position, now they had to wait for the convoy. With the position secure and the members of B company strategically placed the main objective was complete. They stayed in position and continued to come under attack from small arms and RPGs, absorbing the enemy attacks and suppressing them with returning fire.

Pte Robb continued: "The Taliban, up to this time had been a sloppy shot. In the past they tended to hold their rifles up and just shoot them over the top of walls, or around corners without looking. But this time they were taking a bit more time. Although still not accurate they were attempting to take aim as if they had been preparing for this operation and had been training."

By 1500 hrs, seven hours after they had set out in the morning, the convoy made it through. Now the objective was extract back to the outpost. They were aware of what they had come up against on their way out and were prepared for the same on the return leg. " It took us up to an hour to extract back, and again we were under constant attack by the Taliban. Pte Robb concluded: "We wanted to push forward and suppress the Taliban, but knew that the objective was to extract back and do so without taking casualties.

"I had fired off ten magazines – about 300 rounds – and an AT4 (Anti-Tank) missile throughout the day, many of my mates did the same some more, it was awesome. We had achieved the mission aim, given the Taliban a very bloody nose and got back without sustaining any casualties. Afghanistan was brilliant. It's exactly what I joined up for, it was an awesome experience and much better than sitting back home. This was the real thing."

The Guns of 7 Para RHA test firing at camp Bastion.

Gunners of I Battery, 7 Para RHA, in the infantry role at Gereshk.

CHAPTER SEVEN
→ **ARTILLERY ACTION**

Battery Commander, Major Gary Wilkinson, centre, with his Tac HQ at Sangin.

Light Gun detachment at COP Robinson.

//ARTILLERY ACTION
//7th PARACHUTE REGT RHA

The Light Guns arrived in Afghanistan ready to go into action, but with no clear indication that they would actually fire. However, artillery support was to play a key role in the tactical success achieved by the UK Task Force in the months ahead. The Regiment's primary focus on deployment was the specialist training packages for the Afghan National Army as well as the administration command of Camp Bastion. In addition the Regiment was to command and direct a Joint Effects Cell, direct Aviation firepower and other weapons platforms as well support the Force Protection team at Bastion. These tasks would stretch the unit's capability, but by the end of the tour the guns of I Battery, Bull's Troop had fired more than 4,000 rounds of 105mm ammunition. The unit's commanding officer, Lt Col David Hammond, described the tour as 'a challenging operation which demanded significant risk to achieve the mission'.

During the early stages of the deployment, the 3 PARA Battle Group had sufficient resources in order to achieve the effect that they required. However, as the Taliban activities increased, a troop from I Battery was required to revert back to its primary role and deploy from Camp Bastion to provide enduring indirect fire support to troops located at Sangin.

I Para Battery was at the very forefront of the delivery of fire support, commanded by Major Gary Wilkinson RHA. I Para Battery provided 105mm indirect fire from the Light Gun and Fire Support Teams (FSTs) to deliver what is known as the Joint Fires (the term used to describe the different types of weapons whose fire the FSTs directed in support of operations) across Helmand. I Para Battery was 155 men strong, and included a significant RAF element, without which the delivery of all Joint Fires and Battlespace Management would not have been possible. The gun troops provided critical indirect fires during numerous intense engagements with the Taliban, and fired 485 observed fire missions – with a very large proportion of these being inside the Danger Close distances. In addition to providing indirect fires for Coalition Forces the I Para Battery Gun Group also fired 105mm missions in defence of their own gun position on more than one occasion; including direct fire. Bull's Troop's six Light Guns fired 4,053 rounds of ammunition; over 3,000 of which were HE. The impact of the 105mm firepower often proved to have a greater psychological effect on the enemy than air and aviation fire. On one occasion it was the 'weapon of choice' by Coalition Special Forces during an operation. Despite the ammunition expenditure many fire missions only required a small number of rounds to achieve the necessary effect. This was also used in tandem with the key counter-insurgency principle of minimum force. The Light Gun troops were deployed to static locations and also operated in a manoeuvre role alongside 3 PARA Patrols Platoon and the HCR. The special assets such as the Desert Hawk mini-unmanned aerial vehicle operated by 32 Regiment RA, for the first time on operations, proved a great success.

This unique shot of a 105 light gun was taken during a fire mission on Operation HERRICK.

The I Para Battery Gun Group also found themslves deployed in the infantry role on a number of occasions. This loss of offensive support capability was a necessity given the shortfall of infantry troops against the increasing tasks that had to be executed by the troops in Helmand during the early stages of the operation, before additional infantry troops from the Royal Irish and Royal Regiment of Fusiliers arrived. Soldiers and officers from I Para Battery operated as the third rifle platoon in A Company based in Gereshk at the very start of the tour and undertook the identical demanding tasks as the two dedicated rifle platoons of A Company 3 PARA. The Battery also generated two infantry platoons for the force protection of Camp Bastion, which included the WMIK-mounted patrolling of its external area of operations. In Musa Qaleh, during almost three weeks in the dedicated infantry role alongside the Pathfinder Platoon, a platoon formed from I Para Battery fired more than 10,000 small arms rounds and 76 x 40mm SA80 under-slung grenades during intense infantry engagements with the Taliban. They were also, in the early stage of the tour, supported by US 105mm Lt Gun fires when in contact. The I Para Battery infantry patrols also worked alongside ANA patrols in Musa Qaleh under

the guidance of 7 Para RHA OMLT commanders such as Lt James Higgins RHA. I Para Battery supported every 3 PARA Battle Group operation. This normally comprised 1 or 2 troops of 105 mm Light Guns firing in direct support and up to six Fire Support Teams each of six personnel who directed all Joint Fires (mortars, artillery, close air support and close combat attack, from Apache helicopters). These teams proved their worth repeatedly throughout the tour.

The FSTs terminally guided 249 close air support bombs onto Taliban positions, as well as numerous strafing runs from aircraft including 105mm fires from AC-130 Spectre gunships. 3 PARA's support weapons were highly effective; and integrated into the Joint Fires planning of Bull's Troop's FSTs in support of CO 3 PARA's plans. 0.50 cal Browning heavy machine gun and anti-tank missiles were put to good use; fully integrated into all Joint Fires planning and execution. Both MILAN and the new JAVELIN anti-tank missile were taken and used on a number of occasions with excellent results. Over 8,000 rounds of 81mm mortar ammunition were directed, down to distances of 50m, and routinely fired from inside company locations, which allowed even closer proximity.

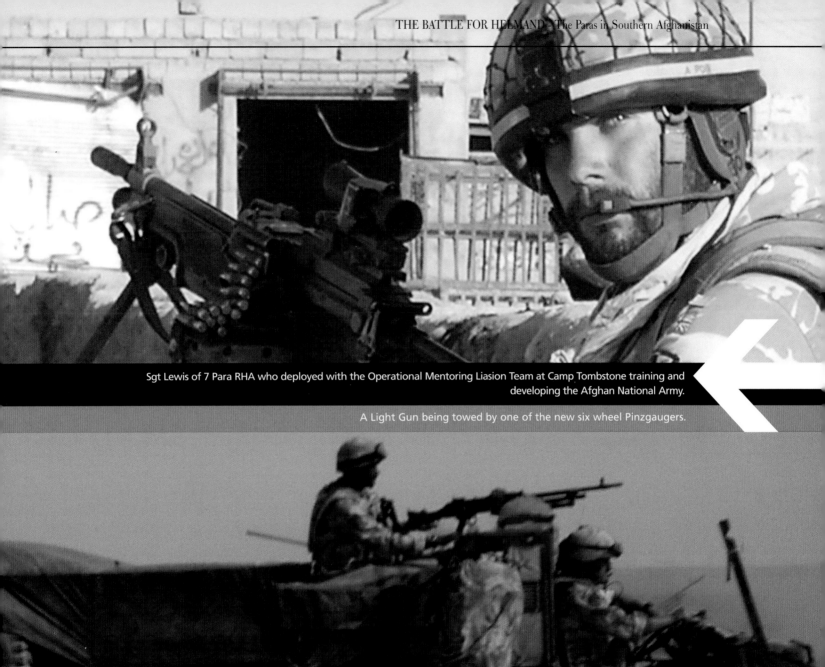

Sgt Lewis of 7 Para RHA who deployed with the Operational Mentoring Liasion Team at Camp Tombstone training and developing the Afghan National Army.

A Light Gun being towed by one of the new six wheel Pinzgaugers.

Close Air Support (CAS) played a major part in many operations and was used predominantly to destroy insurgent positions during contact, in addition to remaining airborne during vulnerable phases of Battle group operations. Thirteen Joint Tactical Attack Controllers (JTACs) were fielded which was rarely enough given the mission-critical nature of these personnel. The JTACs operated either embedded within a Fire Support Team and infantry company, or independently to support a convoy move for example. The JTACs belonging to I Para Battery directed 249 Close Air Support bombs during the tour and were drawn from the HCR, 7 Para RHA, 4/73 Battery RA, 3 PARA and the RAF Regiment.

Sadly along with the successes, the Regiment experienced tragedies. Capt Jim Philippson was killed in a firefight with the Taliban while serving with the OMLT and I Para Battery officer Capt Alex Eida RHA was killed whilst commanding his FST in an ambush near Musa Qaleh. I Battery also suffered two soldiers very seriously wounded in action during the tour.

Lieutenant Colonel David Hammond RHA, added: "The operation has been demanding and challenging and has often involved significant risk to achieve the mission. This has entailed the tragic loss of two fine young officers and a number of serious injuries. The bravery and commitment displayed has been truly remarkable and humbling. The paradigm for which we, as the Royal Artillery within all arms formations, conduct operations has fundamentally altered."

A Light Gun is pictured during a night fire mission.

Captain Armstrong calling in 'a danger close artillery' fire mission at Sangin.

105 mm Light Gun firing illumination rounds during a night mission.

Lieutenant Colonel David Hammond, CO 7 Para RHA.

109

A Scimitar of the Household Cavalry caught on camera as it returns fire during a Taliban attack on Sangin.

Fitted with a metal cage of protection to prevent RPGs detonating on the vehicle a Scimitar moves at speed across the open desert.

CHAPTEREIGHT
→ COMBAT POWER

Troopers from the Household Cavalry pictured at Sangin District Centre.

//COMBAT POWER
//D SQUADRON, HCR

D Squadron, The Household Cavalry, arrived in the blistering heat and began preparing for operations. The first few days were spent planning at Bastion with Battle Group Headquarters and Kandahar where the Brigade Headquarters was located. This allowed the command group to link up with the pilots from the RAF who flew many sorties in support of the Household Cavalry Regiment. In order to fully acclimatise and get used to the savagery of operating within the Scimitars at the extreme temperatures, the Squadron took on the task of providing Force Protection (FP) for the Engineers as they repaired the runway. Here the drivers and crews had their first taste of the boiling temperatures inside the vehicles that were to increase in July and August. Initially the Squadron's training serial was cut dramatically short by a task out of area to the east of Lashkar Gah, providing a screen in support of the Regional Task Force (Canadians). In the end the screen task was uneventful with the Canadians frankly stating that the Taliban knew we were coming and did not want to get embroiled in a fight with what they regarded as small tanks. Again the heat took its toll on both vehicles and men, the most serious of which was a near fatality who had an inner core temperature of 41.7 degrees. Two other heat casualties were taken and had to be evacuated using the Immediate Response Team (IRT) based out of a Chinook helicopter escorted by Apache. It soon became apparent to the Squadron that each town boasted a hard core of Taliban fighters, tenacious, extremely courageous often to the point of insanity, persistent and well armed with bountiful ammunition quantities, although many a Quartermaster would have winced at their storage discipline! Initially the enemy had freedom to manoeuvre between the towns, surging in areas across the Sangin valley, they felt they could have an effect. Deliberate operations to deplete their numbers and resupply the District Centres were to become essential tasks as the campaign progressed.

Corporal of Horse Fry LG who was attached to 7 Para Royal Horse Artillery (7 PARA) as a Joint Tactical Air Controller (JTAC) was injured in Sangin and two of the Light Electronic Warfare Team (LEWT) were killed. Fry called in a huge amount of fire from the air, and single handedly covered the extraction of A Company 3 PARA during a raid in Now Zad when twenty one enemy fighters were killed. Despite his wounds, he continued to do his job and called in a B1B to drop 500lb bombs on Taliban positions – all in all a huge credit to the Regiment.

On the initial move form Gereshk to Sangin the convoy was attacked by an IED (Improvised Explosive Device). The last vehicle in the convoy, an Afghan National Police truck carrying four soldiers, was destroyed killing all its occupants and wounding a further three. The vehicle was only 30 yards behind the rear lorry, a REME vehicle. Following the operation 2 Troop were left in Sangin to provide force protection for the Engineer teams that remained to improve the District Centre defences and perimeter. They ended up staying there until mid August, almost five weeks in duration - having packed for a six day recce! Shortly afterwards the Squadron rapidly deployed to Now Zad to take much needed ammunition to D Company stationed there, following reports of a heavy machine gun being seen in the area and therefore it not being safe to fly the ammunition up via support helicopter. Now Zad had been a hot bed of activity with the Gurkhas having exchanged hand grenades across the wall with the Taliban at times. Following a period of patrolling in the town the squadron closed down the enemy attacks. This was followed by a 3 PARA operation to relieve the Gurkhas with C Company 3 PARA in which Scimitars engaged targets in depth in support of infantry on the ground. Unfortunately, there was no time to cement this position, as Brigade ordered D Squadron and the Gun Group to Musa Qaleh.

Scimitar deployed across Helmand to support 3 PARA patrols on the ground.

This was the precursor to the most significant action of the Squadron's tour, as 1 Troop was left behind in Now Zad to support C Company while the remainder pushed toward Musa Qaleh escorting elements of I Battery 7 Para RHA, and ordered to have a diversionary effect in support of an extraction plan for the Danish Recce Coy and Pathfinders who required to relocate from Musa Qaleh. Once the guns were in position the Scimitars pushed forward in an attempt to get eyes onto Musah Qaleh from the ridgeline to the west of the town. Initially, minefields and fog hampered this and one Scimitar struck an anti-tank mine. The explosion caused significant damage to the vehicle; this included the destruction of the running gear, the removal of the engine decks, and the loss of the gear box and buckling of the vehicle's chassis. Fortunately and testament to the new mine blast protection fitted to the vehicle, Corporal of Horse Moses of the Life Guards and the remainder of his crew were unharmed. The vehicle was subsequently destroyed using Apache Hellfire missiles (the bombing procedures ensured that the enemy could not get access to the remains of the vehicle or anything in it). Following the mine strike, the Squadron manoeuvred to try and achieve their mission but tragically were caught in a well coordinated Taliban ambush. The initial command wire operated IED destroyed callsign 41, killing 2Lt Ralph Johnson LG, Captain Alex Eida 7 Para RHA and LCpl Ross Nicholls RHG/D immediately.

CoH Flynn RHG/D with his crew of Tpr Minter RHG/D and Tpr Leach RHG/D were caught in the ambush killing area their path out blocked forward and back. They managed to extract themselves under heavy enemy fire back to the relative safety of other vehicles. LCoH Radford showed tremendous bravery moving forward into the killing area to extract an injured colleague with the aide of cover from CoH Flynn and 3 Troop callsigns. This action was extremely intense, with the Taliban attempting to cut off significant numbers of vehicles and troops, defeated only by the initiative of LCoH Anderson RHG/D using the 51mm mortar to great effect. The Immediate Reaction Team (IRT) and CO's Tactical Headquarters were quickly deployed.

A memorial service was subsequently held back at Bastion, hugely supported by the Battle Group, especially by 3 PARA HQ. The soldiers were repatriated back to the UK via Kandahar where over 1,000 members of ISAF paid their respects. The Squadron was given a short amount of time to reflect before pushing on, with more deliberate operations into Musa Qaleh and Now Zad. In these operations the anti-tank weapon Milan was fired for the first time having been mounted on Spartan to give it more punch!

The re-supplying of the outstations was becoming increasingly difficult, especially around Musa Qaleh and Sangin. The threat to aviation assets had risen dramatically and a Chinook had taken direct hits from small arms fire. This had a knock on effect to our outstation support as vehicles requiring much needed spares were remaining off the road as they could not be brought forward in a timely fashion. Whilst the troops did their best to maintain the fleet, the lack of spares through the system was also further affecting our capabilities, which was to be a reoccurring theme throughout the tour. Only twice did we deploy from Bastion without a vehicle or more breaking down due to automotive problems before we had reached the A1 road, not more than 6 kms from the camp. However as the heat died down in late August and early September improvements to the vehicles reliability started to pick up. A Relief in Place (RIP) of Now Zad could be easily achieved and often we would do a sub unit move to accomplish this.

This gave the CVR(T) fleet the ability to rotate through this static location thereby changing vehicles and crews. This was not possible in Sangin although a RIP of troops was completed by helicopter, following the tragic death of LCpl Tansey who died in a repair accident. The Squadron, less the vehicles awaiting parts (always two or more), were more frequently being used to test the 'Manoeuvre Outreach Group' (MOG) theory. This involved deploying into the wider expanses of the desert to dominate the ground, and transit routes, but also to allow for more interaction with the local populous. When given the right assets, this worked well and we were often used to great effect between Musa Qaleh and Now Zad.

The largest threat to the Squadron and MOG Group came from mines that had either washed down the wadis or from legacy mines that littered the desert. Unfortunately they were often difficult or impossible to spot. The Squadron and 3 PARA patrols platoon suffered six mine strikes between them, the most serious of which destroyed a WMIK providing flank protection as part of one of our convoys. All three of the occupants survived, although a solider from 7 Para RHA, was injured. Again the IRT, ambulance crew and other members of the MOG performed admirably to ensure they survived and were extracted to safety at the field hospital in a timely manner. CoH Hoggarth LG and his crew had a lucky escape four days later when their CVR(T) triggered an anti tank mine on the extremities of the track, blowing the bar armour off and disabling the vehicle in a vulnerable Taliban area.

Inside the busy hospital at Camp Bastion.

A Sapper from 2 Troop mans the 50 Cal at Sangin.

CHAPTERNINE
→ THE SPECIALISTS

The Recce Platoon of 51 Parachute Squadron RE

Building the sangars, often under fire.

//THE SPECIALISTS
//ENGINEERS IN THE FRONT LINE

The newly named 51 Parachute Squadron Royal Engineers deployed to Helmand province tasked with providing combat engineering support to 3 PARA Battle Group. Operating as a Group with the support of a field troop from 9 Para Squadron, two WMIK (Land Rover) based recce teams from 12 HQ Squadron, a total of 161 airborne sappers arrived in southern Afghanistan. Within weeks the Battle Group became decisively engaged in counter insurgency and Operations in Built Up Area (OBUA). The Group supported all operations and after the troop reinforcement of the District Centres was called upon to reinforce these locations against attack. The Squadron Group supported the Battle Group on six separate deliberate war fighting operations; operating as infantry sections and providing explosive entry where required. The culmination of which resulted in the Squadron Group fortifying the Sangin District Centre (now known as FOB Jackson in recognition of the late Pte Jackson) and constructing an Air Portable Ferry Bridge (APFB) in the River Helmand, despite accurate and sustained enemy fire. All told an exceptionally kinetic operational tour. In total 78 barmines were fired in anger to deny vehicles and destroy buildings, in some cases they were used as mouse hole charges. In Sangin the walls were up to eight foot thick.

The town of Sangin was the location of the first six UK deaths in Helmand Province and when 2 Troop were deployed to the District Centre in the town at short notice to provide vital protection to support B Company 3 PARA. They knew it would be an extremely volatile and dangerous environment and within an hour of arrival they witnessed their first encounter with the Taliban as small arms, RPGs and 107mm rockets rained down onto the compound. The defences were skeleton, and 2 Troop arrived with 20,000 sandbags, two kilometres of wire coil, 400 six ft pickets and several tonnes of enthusiasm, to improve the defences. Progress was slow under constant enemy fire with enemy rounds landing at the feet of sappers laying freshly filled sandbags. The provision of defences, primarily sangars, (defensive Observation Posts) and wire obstacles, went well, despite the constant fire fights. As the attacks increased A10 and B1 air support became a nightly event and numerous firing points were denied to the enemy with the use of 500lb JDAMs and the deployment of 3 Troops's bar mines.

The situation worsened and Sangin became the Battle Group main effort. A Battle Group operation was launched into Sangin, and the whole of 51 Parachute Squadron (Gp) was deployed in high risk search operations and mobility support in the form of heavy mouse hole charges. The Battle Group dominated the ground and with a huge convoy of stores, 51 Parachute Squadron Gp began the construction of Forward Operating Base Jackson. The construction began with a three kilometre double storey HESCO perimeter wall built under a constant barrage of RPG and small arms fire. In order to protect engineer manpower, a Gun Group, manned by the Squadron and armed with .50 Cal HMG and GPMGs, was established. This proved invaluable and the Gun Group found themselves putting down massive amounts of fire, four or five times a day, in order to allow the workforce to get into cover.

SSgt Bruce Dickinson of 3 Troop, 9 Para Squadron recalls his experience at Musa Qaleh. He said: "In August the Squadron Group supported a two company deliberate operation in the area of Musa Qaleh which saw the logistics resupply of the bases as well as the insertion of Danish Recce. Orders began two days before, and meant a day of making up mousehole charges for the troop. With two charges carried per man and a reserve on the CSM's quad, the troop was again divided a section each to B and C Companies of 3 PARA. We were all flown by Chinook in two waves to a HLS (Helicopter Landing Site) about 1 Kilometre away from our objective and then tabbed (walked at speed) to an FUP (Forming Up Position) where we assumed assault formation. The objective was for each company to clear a number of compounds either side of the MSR (Main Supply Route) and then clear a 300 metre green zone of orchards and fields to ensure the safe passage of vehicles across the wadi. Bayonets were fixed, and behind a rolling barrage of artillery and mortars, we advanced down the hill and into the compounds, the mouse hole charges sounding like artillery landing too close for comfort! The enemy compounds were all found to be empty, having been treated to an evening of artillery and JDAMs delivered by B1 bombers. There was sporadic gunfire as the Canadian LAVs (Light Armoured Vehicles) moved out to secure the wadi, however Pathfinders were soon driving through the cleared route under the watchful eye of two Apache helicopters. The resupply then went in successfully, however tragically resulting in the death of a logistic force protection platoon top gunner due to enemy small arms fire. The manoeuvre elements then moved back to the HLS to fly back, literally just in time, for our evening meal in Camp Bastion"

In one of the Squadron's final operations they deployed and constructed, under fire, an Air Portable Ferry Bridge (APFB) by the field troop from 9 Parachute Squadron. Sappers were to fly into an area near Sangin and then link up with a convoy carrying the bridge. Cpl Lovegrove of 3 Troop 9 Para Squadron recounts his experience.

He said: "Two Minutes, was passed down the aircraft, to alert everyone that we were about to land – everyone was already on their feet, facing the rear, and poised ready to go! My section, having only recently returned from Sangin, was expecting 'incoming fire' straight away. They were focussed and ready for the job in hand - to rendezvous with the rest of our troop, wait for a road convoy to arrive and construct the all-new Air Portable Ferry Bridge (APFB).

"Standby, standby and before you could blink we were down the tail ramp and out into all-round defence along with CO 3 PARA's TAC (Tactical headquarters). C Company 3 PARA moved off to the south east and within minutes the first contacts were heard as 2 Troop started mouse holing (explosive charges) their way through compounds to secure their objective. Major Warhurst set off towards the District Centre with my section giving support from the rear. Once in the District Centre LCpl Brookes was there to meet us and give us a quick brief. Suddenly an RPG hit the wall within the compound just metres from where we were stood. Contacts then started as B Company with 2 Troop moved to their objective in the north. The convoy had finally arrived and Apache's were giving overhead protection so we started to move back to the compound.

"SSgt Bruce Dickson, Sgt Eddie Edwards, Cpl Damo Parsons and his section had been stripping out the pallets carrying the bridge and started constructing the launching frame. As they did they took incoming fire from the tree line 200 metres to the south. So with rounds 'zipping over their heads' and the HCR suppressing the enemy fire with their Scimitar's 30mm Radon Cannon and five Milan missiles they carried on building the bridge. The whole troop was now on the bridge site and so with Cpl Parsons on the left of the bridge, myself on the right and LCpl Foley in the centre, we started the construction, it was 1530 hrs. The bridge went a lot easier than expected, very unusual, and so by 1900 hrs the ferry bridge was sat on the water ready to go. At first light we moved down to the bridge, it was time to 'prove' the crossing, then make sure it was ready for heavy loads."

Royal Enginers deliver the last few sections of the ferry bridge during Operation BAGHI.

Reinforcing Sangin Distcrict Centre was a challenging and very dangerous task for 51 Squadron.

Sappers reinforce a sangar observation post.

Major Chris Warhurst briefs his men at Sangin.

//THE SPECIALISTS
//SAPPERS AT WORK

The Royal Engineers of 51 Parachute Squadron deployed on almost every operation in southern Afghanistan delivering a wide range of skills from combat engineer, to bomb disposal and engineer reconnaissance. At Musa Qaleh, Sangin, Now Zad, Gereshk and Kajaki sappers were flown in to reinforce the District Centres against enemy attack. Often under fire they built protective walls, erected sand bagged outposts. In one unique operation they deployed and erected a ferry bridge, while under fire.

During all operations it was Royal Engineers who spearheaded the advance by clearing the ground of mines and any obstacles. During one Battle Group mission at Musa Qaleh the engineers moved forward to mark a clear path though an area of trees and vegetation known as 'the green zone'. The bomb disposal officer and his team found two significant Improvised Explosive Devices (IED), which they neutralised. When rockets were fired at District Centres and failed to detonate it was a Royal Engineer officer who was again called into inspect the munitions and make it safe.

Sappers worked at every location across Helmand to reinforce the District Centres.

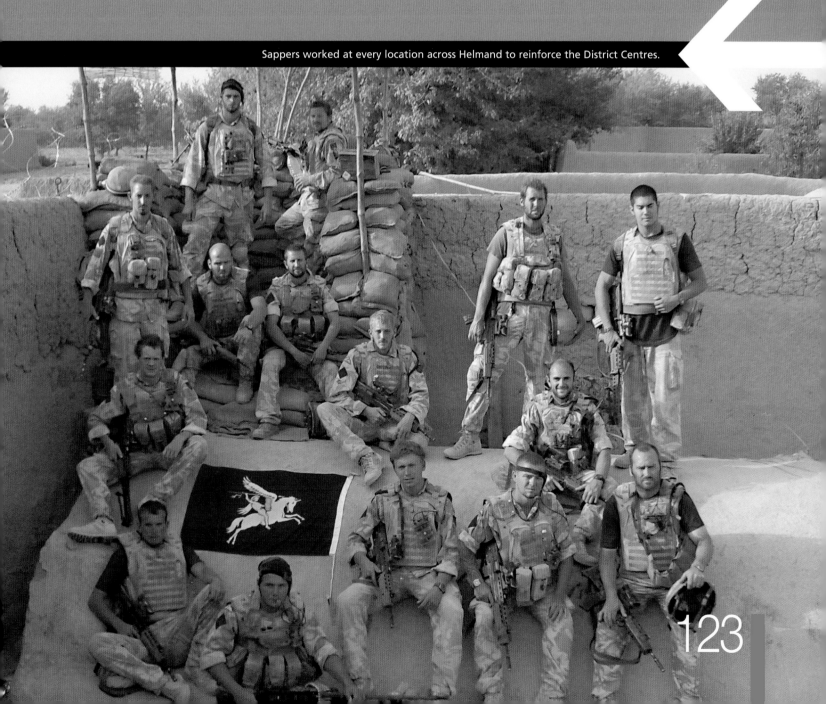

Where possible medical aid was given to the local population.

Inside the hospital, described by one patient as very busy and very professional.

//THE SPECIALISTS
//JOINT FORCE MEDICAL GROUP

The months prior to deployment were hectic as 16 Close Support Medical Regiment prepared for operations in southern Afghanistan. Once in Camp Bastion the medics were immersed in an operational tempo, which was far higher than anyone could have predicted. The Regiment joined with a Hospital Squadron from 22 Field Hospital to form the Joint Force Medical Group. In addition the wartime establishment was achieved by bringing in individuals from all three Services in a process that worked well.

Among the first elements from the Brigade to deploy, M Section arrived in Camp Bastion in early February to provide medical support to 39 Engineer Regiment who were tasked with constructing Camp Bastion. During pre-deployment at Lydd in Kent staff had described Camp Bastion as austere and it was never more so than when the advance elements of the unit arrived. When more of the Medical Group arrived in late March and early April, M Section moved across to Lashkar Gah in order to support the Provincial Reconstruction Team who were patrolling from that location. It was in the provincial capital on Good Friday that one of their own team was injured in an explosion caused by a suicide car bomber. The Medical Group had been given a harsh introduction to operating in Helmand Province before the Main Body had even arrived in theatre.

Early tasks for the Medical Group included completing and staffing the Role 2 Enhanced Field Hospital which had an emergency capacity of up to 50 beds, providing medical support to the outstations at Lashkar Gah and Forward Operating Base Price near Gereshk as well as to the Pathfinder Platoon who operated just about everywhere.

In addition the Group contributed to the Immediate Response Team capability, which consisted of an on-call medical team ready to deploy aboard a Chinook anywhere across Helmand in support of seriously inured soldiers. The emergency bed capacity was prepared for, but no one could have realised that the first Mass Casualty Situation would happen so soon. It was declared when a French Embedded Training Team/Afgan National Army call-sign was ambushed between Sangin and Kajaki which resulted in the largest single Immediate Response Team callout with 24 casualties (the majority of which were gun shot wounds) arriving at the accident and emergency department at the same time. It was a major challenge, which the Group rose to.

As the mission in Helmand Province developed the medics expanded their support to include more Combat Outposts as they were occupied. By the halfway point of the operation the Joint Medical Group had deployed a Medical Section each to Forward Operating Base (FOB) Price and Lashkar Gah, a Doctor and Combat Medical Technician (CMT) to Combat Outpost (COP) Jackson in Sangin, a Doctor and CMT to Now Zad, a Doctor to Musa Qaleh, two CMTs to Kajaki, two for COP Robinson, with a CMT continuing to support the Pathfinder Platoon. Intermittently the Group also provided personnel to support the Household Cavalry, 13 Regiment Royal Logistics Corps for large convoys, the Operational Mentor and Liaison Team (OMLT) and the Danish Contingent while they were in Musa Qaleh. Further support in Sangin and Musa Qaleh was provided by 3 PARA Regimental Aid Post (RAP).

Casualties are taken from a Chinook at Camp Bastion to be transferred to the hospital.

The Regimental Aid Post was bolstered by the Medical Group during all major operations. In addition they also provided individual replacements to the 3 PARA Battle Group as infantrymen, radio operators and Combat Infantry Medics. FOB Price proved to be an interesting location for the Medical Section posted there because as well as providing primary healthcare for the population and supporting the patrols framework of the 3 PARA Rifle Company, they were also called upon to help manage the Host Nation Clinic which was there for use by Local Nationals and provided considerable variation in cases.

At Lashkar Gah the Medical Section supported the Provincial Reconstruction Teams operations. They were the first responding call-sign to the Hercules C130 which crashed during landing and was destroyed on Bost Airfield. Those medics posted to COP Jackson treated casualties of some of the worst fighting the Task Force saw in Helmand Province while those in Now Zad and Musa Qaleh dealt with the victims of daily attritional small arms shoots and indirect fire attacks.

Where Combat Medical Technicians operated without the support of Medical Officers they were often required to work to the full extent of their capabilities and regularly surpassed their skill sets, often under contact. In all locations Medics were also challenged with providing care for the ANA and ANP. On occasion there was also call to treat Local Nationals with the need to comply whenever possible with Muslim Custom, especially when treating women.

At the time the Medical Group completed its tour, the Field Hospital had treated in excess of 1,000 casualties not including more than 150 WIA. Behind the scenes the Medical Group contributed to the sustainability of the mission by providing dental, physio and psychological care on demand as well as Environmental Health through water testing and pest control. Close communication with 3 PARA Battle Group was maintained by Medical Liaison Officers working in the Joint Operations Centre at Bastion who helped link IRT call-signs with the hospital when casualties were taken on the ground and provided a centre of gravity for medical information for the Province.

The Casualty

LCpl Cook is just one example of the many casualties who received treatment at Camp Bastion. A member of 216 Air Assault Signals Squadron he was shot and injured coming down the steps of an improvised sangar position at the Platoon House in the town of Now Zad. He had just finished repairing a field telephone line that had been hit by enemy sniper fire, when further shots were fired. As he was moving into cover inside the compound his Detachment Commander, Cpl Steel, noticed that he had blood running from underneath his Combat Body Armour. LCpl Cook had not even noticed that he had been hit, but on removing his Combat Body Armour and shirt, it was discovered that a 7.62 bullet had entered his back and just missed his vital organs. With two entry wounds and one exit wound, LCpl Cook lost a fair amount of blood, but was not in a life threatening condition. He was med-evaced to Camp Bastion where he received the best available care. According to his colleagues he has been left with some sizeable battle scars, as the bullet was difficult to locate. The round recovered from his back has been made into a 'special' necklace, and his shirt has been framed with a photograph of him with his detachment and presented to the Squadron. LCpl Cook is pictured right and the X-ray shows the bullet head.

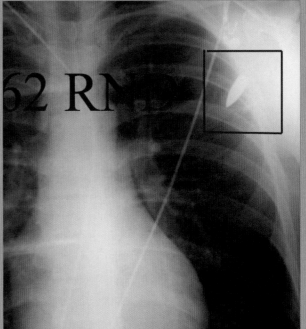

A medic from 16 Close Support Regiment gives life saving treatment to a soldier from the Afghan National Army during the battle for Garmser.

A Royal Military Police patrol in Lashkar Gah.

A RMP solder mans the gun at Sangin.

//THE SPECIALISTS
//156 PROVOST COMPANY RMP

In April 2006, 1 Platoon from 156 Provost Company Royal Military Police deployed to Helmand Province in Close Support to the 3 PARA Battle Group. The small unit was to be totally embedded with the Battle Group with military policemen on the ground working alongside the infantry. A package of rigorous re-deployment training was undertaken in order that all members of the section could operate on the ground and use all the section weapons, particularly the heavy machine gun which some soldiers would find themselves manning during the tour. This tour was to be historic for military police operations in that they were totally integrated into the Battle Group and the experience and lessons learned would potentially change the style of training and operations for The Red Caps in the future.

RMP personnel supported every operation carried out by 3 PARA BG and in addition military policemen were embedded within the Company Groups and deployed on the ground in Sangin, Musa Qaleh and Now Zad District Centres. Deployed personnel were routinely co-located with the Company Sergeant Major or Tactical Headquarters. On other occasions they deployed with the forward companies. The Platoon also supported framework patrols from Forward Operating Base (FOB) Price at Gereshk.

Within the RMP platoon there was limited operational experience. The majority had never experienced an operational tour before let alone one involving such close combat. Iraq has toughened up the RMP to a point where it is almost unrecognisable from the relative safety of its past. But Iraq is predominately a vehicle mounted operation, southern Afghanistan was not. Operating in temperatures upwards of 40°C and carrying in excess of 25kg of equipment, Helmand was challenging without the Taliban. The issue of L109 HE grenades and L84 RP grenades as well as 500 rounds of 5.56 ammunition focussed the minds of most members of the platoon. On returning to Camp Bastion much of this load was often expended, generating a fast and furious introduction to close combat for the platoon and experience for the future.

The initial reservations of the rifle companies of having two military police Corporals with them was quickly dismissed following either a contact or a situation where police support was necessary immediately. Platoon personnel attended a number of incidents during the deployment, in all of the locations resulting in a quick and seamless recovery of evidence.

These ranged from photographs taken at the scene of a shooting incident, to recovery of prisoners taken during an operation to the investigation into the death of British soldiers and examination of the scene. Some of these investigations were carried out under fire and the personal courage of the men in the platoon as well as the high quality of advice and product delivered to the BG was praised. Instead of the delay in calling members of the platoon into the field to investigate an incident at which personnel would arrive after it had happened and need a detailed brief, they were already there. This new format generated confidence within the platoon and won respect from the paratroopers they served with. But most importantly the integration allowed RMP staff to gain a better understating of the situation on the ground and when required, to investigate with a much deeper appreciation of the incident.

As the tour came to an end Brigadier Ed Butler, the commander of 16 Air Assault Brigade and the UK Task Force in Helmand told the platoon 'You are at the cutting edge of military policing, during the fight of our generation, be proud of your achievements, but do not rest on your laurels'

Back in Colchester clear changes to the platoon's daily business were planned. Battle PT, load bearing marches and weapon handling are all now commonplace within the Company lines at 156 Provost.

The extreme heat and demanding work punished the vehicles.

REME Mechanics often found themselves repairing vehicles and then engaged in firefights.

//THE SPECIALISTS
//8 CS TROOP, 7 BATTALION REME

The deployment of 8 Close Support Troop, 7 Air Assault battalion Royal Electrical Mechanical Engineers. to southern Afghanistan highlighted that every member of the REME is a soldier first and a tradesman second. This was extremely apparent when Sgt Western and Craftsman Brannigan briefly joined the Pathfinder Group. Having completed a clutch change on a WMIK Land Rover they found themselves fighting alongside the Pathfinders in a running battle against the Taliban.

The initial task of the REME in Afghanistan was the Ballistic Protection Enhancement modification of all Brigade vehicles in theatre. In addition Sgt Davidson played a key role in establishing the repair facility which ensured rapid turnaround of damaged modules, guaranteeing that maximum protection was provided to the troops on the ground.

Due to the high intensity of the operations being conducted and the significant amount of ammunition being expended, the armourers, and namely Sgt Whatling, were critical in enabling units to bring to bear a maximum weight of firepower, at all times. This, despite the destruction, by the Taliban, of Sgt Whatling's vehicle and all weapons spares in it!.

The recovery mechanics found themselves consistently busy. All resupply convoys required recovery assets and support, which provided these teams with then unenviable opportunity of visiting every outpost in Helmand from Sangin to Musa Qaleh. Additionally a Samson recovery crew was detached to D Squadron, Household Cavalry and its crew was involved in numerous firefights. LCpl Cording spent 27 days of his 28, in Sangin Platoon House, in contact with the enemy, again highlighting the soldier first priority. To his credit Cpl Burton showed commendable dexterity in keeping the HCR's tracked vehicles moving despite regular breakdowns through overheating and gearbox failures, ensuring minimal loss of operational momentum.

The recovery of vehicles was difficult and in the main those damaged were bombed.

WARNING
HOT
DO NOT TOUCH

The food delivered by the RLC was of a amazing standard, particularly as the chefs were working in such extreme heat conditions.

Helicopters were used on a daily basis to push supplies of food and ammunition forward to the frontline.

132

CHAPTER TEN
→ SUSTAINING THE FORCE

A paratrooper stands guard as an RLC convoy arrives to re-supply a District Centre.

Scimitars escort a major RLC supply convoy out of Camp Bastion.

134

//SUSTAINING THE FORCE
//13 AIR ASSAULT REGT RLC

The planning and preparation for the deployment of 13 Air Assault Regiment, Royal Logistics Corps, started in early October with a series of meetings with 16 Air Assault Brigade, Land Command and the Permanent Joint Headquarters. The aim was to identify the level of support required to the Brigade, the manpower and equipment requirements to carry out the mission as well as the deployment timeframes. Those warned off for operations comprised; 24 HQ Squadron including RHQ, 15 Squadron, 82 General Support Squadron and 1 Troop from 63 Air Assault Squadron. In theatre the Regiment would take under command 8 Close Support Squadron from 7 Air Assault Battalion REME, 84 Medical Squadron and the Postal and Courier Troop. After much packing, training and pre-deployment exercises alongside the Battle Group the advance units left in February. 82 General Support (GS) Squadron and elements of the Quartermaster's department deployed to Kandahar. A larger contingent followed in March and by early April most of the RLC personnel and resources had arrived with 15 Squadron (CS) who were to act as the close support to 3 PARA Battle Group being based in Camp Bastion. The UK logistics force operated from Kandahar, Bastion and Kabul with independent support to Gereshk and Lashkar Gah. The deployment of troops to secure the District Centre would also require logistical support.

The Air Despatch team from 47 AD undertook the first UK Air Despatch in Afghanistan delivering four one-ton containers of water to troops deployed in the Sangin District Centre.

The first significant task for the battalion operating out of Bastion was a re-supply to Sangin District Centre in July. The convoy consisted of over 50 vehicles including DROPS (Demountable Rack Offload and Pickup System) and Engineer vehicles. Force Protection Troop provided support in WMIK with the Household Cavalry under battalion command to provide flank protection. The convoy successfully delivered the much-needed combat supplies to the deployed troops and the following day an air despatch of over 30 pallets was dropped into FOB Robinson. In order to maintain supplies a number of road moves were mounted between Kandahar and the key locations. Two further operations were conduced in August. The first was Op SNAKEBITE, a re-supply of combat supplies into the District Centre at Musa Qaleh. It was during this operation that Private Andrew Cutts, of the Force Protection Troop, was killed during the extraction phase of the mission. During the tour the Battalion issued 1.7 million rounds of various ammunitions and explosives, 82,400 rations, half a million liters of water, 5.4 million liters of fuel and 5,600 containers of oils and industrial gas in addition to some 20,000 receipts of materiel from the UK.

Soldiers from the Force Protection Troop man machine guns mounted to the cab of re-supply trucks at Musa Qaleh.

Force Protection Troop had to come to terms with the tragic loss of Pte Cutts and the strong bond between all the soldiers enabled them to bounce back. Pte Leonard, deployed as a radio operator with the Force Protection Troop. He recalls: "I was informed of 13 Air Assault Support Regiment's impending deployment in September 2005. Force Protection Troop was formed to support logistic convoys through Helmand Province and Kandahar. Training began almost immediately, incorporating Team Medics, aggressive driving and how to dominate the road, and also weapon training with the SA80, pistol, Minimi, GPMG, 51 mm Mortar and .50 Calibre HMG.

"After arriving in Helmand our first move consisted of a convoy from Bastion to Lashkar Gah escorting a load of vehicles to the Provincial Reconstruction Team (PRT). This was the first major road move in Helmand, and coupled with the threat of Suicide-Vehicle-Borne Improvised Explosive Device (SVBIED) attacks in the area, I was obviously tense and apprehensive about how the move would develop. The first half of the route was over open desert posing less of a threat, but on entering Lashkar Gah town we soon realised that it was exceedingly busy, even early in the morning. During the move we were supported by an AH-64 Apache, providing top cover and alerting us of any possible obstructions on our chosen route.

"The next convoy we were assigned was the 'big one': Kandahar to Bastion and we were briefed that the chance of being attacked was high. Due to the threat we were told that if we felt our lives were in danger, we were allowed to fire warning shots into the ground. This gave the lads a massive confidence boost as we had been unsure what the consequences would be if we had used warning shots on the first move. Thankfully all went well"

Soldiers from 82 GS Squadron supported the Canadians in their biggest operation against the Taliban. Eight drivers and four DROPS vehicles helped supply the Canadian troops during Operation MEDUSA. The mission saw intense fighting in an area near to Kandahar where more than 1,000 Taliban killed, according to official Canadian statements.

[The DROPS lorry is a huge platform which can carry ammunition and stores around the battlefield and drop them the entire load for troop use. Drops stands for Demountable Rack Offload and Pick Up system].

A Chinook flies low and fast over Helmand. Sand filters can be seen on the intakes to stop damage to the engines from the very fine sand.

RAF Harrier lifts out of Kandahar

138

CHAPTERELEVEN
→ AVIATION SUPPORT

The deployment of the Apache to Afghanistan was fundamental to the success of the troops on the ground.

Ground crew arm an Apache at Camp Bastion.

140

//AVIATION SUPPORT
//THE JOINT HELICOPTER FORCE

The aircrews of the Joint Helicopter Force deployed to southern Afghanistan were well trained and prepared. They knew their aircraft would be fundamental in supporting infantry operations, providing aerial fire support, equipment delivery and casualty evacuation. RAF crews manned the twin rotor Chinook, while the Apache and Lynx helicopters were flown by Army Air Corps pilots. Operating out of Kandahar, aircraft were flown forward to be based at Camp Bastion on a rotation. Chinooks flew in pairs with an Apache in support, watching and waiting for any enemy activity. The Chinook was the workhorse of the Task Force, and throughout the deployment the airframes clocked up hundreds of hours. Known within the military as the Support Helicopter force, their priority role was in support of the Battle Group on operations. But the Chinook crews also provided what was called the Immediate Reaction Team (IRT) which was on call to respond to an incident with extra troops and if required a crew of medics, who on many occasions flew into to rescue a seriously injured soldiers under heavy enemy fire. Chinook pilots spoke of the 'ticking' noise that small arms rounds made as they passed and sometimes hit the fuselage. At Sangin a Chinook crew went into the same landing site three times within one hour at night under heavy fire in order to extract casualties and drop off emergency ammunition. The Apache pilot who was providing cover in an over watch position said that it looked like the closing scene from Star Wars as the Chinook went in and the sky was full of tracer rounds.

The Apache, deployed in Helmand in 2006 for the first time on operations, had been procured by the British Army as an Attack Helicopter to defeat armour. Its lethal weapons and speed allowed the Apache to deliver constant support to the infantry during firefights.

The two crew helicopters were also used to provide top cover for infantry during routine patrols. They shadowed troops during operations and worked as aerial reconnaissance platforms ahead of advancing troops. For soldiers on the ground taking fire from Taliban positions the sight of an Apache above them raised spirits. The 30mm cannon mounted below the Apache's fuselage proved to be a decisive weapon system, engaging enemy forces at the direction of Forward Air Controllers on the ground, at times within metres of UK forces. No other fire support weapon could get as close and have such a devastating effect. The Apache crews were able to bring the 30mm cannon to bear as quickly as a soldier could bring a rifle to his shoulder. Hellfire missiles and CRV7 rockets were used to suppress enemy positions with great success.

The Lynx meanwhile with its speed and handling was often used for evacuating injured soldiers. The twin-engine aircraft was used as a troop carrier and in the medical evacuation role. The courage of the crews cannot be underestimated. At Musa Qaleh District Centre, which came under constant attack a Lynx crew flew in to airlift an injured soldier just after dawn. The Lynx suddenly appeared from nowhere and seemed to make a nosedive landing into the District Centre to the amazement of the soldiers at the base.

Back at Bastion and Kandahar, ground crews worked tirelessly to ensure that the aircraft were constantly serviceable and prepared to fly at short notice. There was no doubt in anyones mind that they did not just fix the helicopters but generated what the military term combat capability. The arming and fuelling teams worked long shifts in the sun, wearing full body armour and grabbing food whenever they could in order to make sure that aircraft could always be refueled and re-armed.

Dust and sand showers a Chinook as it picks up paratroopers after an operation.

An Army Air Corps Lynx lands at the District Centre in Musa Qaleh.

The same aircraft pictured seconds earlier as it appeared to dive into the DC.

//AVIATION SUPPORT
//THE LYNX DROPS IN

These amazing pictures of an Army Air Corps Lynx helicopter were taken at the District Centre in Musa Qaleh. Chinooks had been regularly attacked with rocket-propelled grenades when they swept in to airlift-injured soldiers and, as a result, when the opportunity allowed, a Lynx was sent in. Smaller and very fast the Lynx preferred the cooler air of the early morning, but the risks of flying into the base were still high. In this case a Danish soldier had been shot in the head and needed urgent medical assistance, while another was classified as 'walking wounded' by the medics. According to Danish soldiers in the base, the Lynx almost nosed dived as it flew into Musa Qaleh then swung around at speed and landed. A short period of time on the ground was critical as the risk of a mortar attack was high.

The casualty had been prepared in a stretcher with colleagues waiting to carry him to the aircraft. The courage of the Lynx crew is something that the Danish soldiers will never forget. Their colleague was seriously injured, but thanks to the quick evacuation back to Camp Bastion where he was given vital life saving treatment he made a good recovery. One of the Danish soldiers said: "I will never forget that small helicopter suddenly dropping so fast out of the sky. Several of us thought for a second that he was going to pile in, he was a very good pilot and very brave. I salute him" While different nations believed in their own luck, the Danes believed that the special paint applied to their vehicles was 'lucky paint' and as such it helped protect them! The fact is that despite several serious injuries they did not suffer any fatalities.

The seconds tick by as an injured Danish soldier is loaded into the Lynx.

143

RAF GR7 pictured at Kandahar as the sun goes down.

RAF GR7 lifts out of Kandahar to support ground forces in Helmand.

//AVIATION SUPPORT
//FIXED WING OPERATIONS

The RAF's fast jet fighter support to operations in southern Afghanistan was powerful and contributed significantly to the success of infantry troops on the ground. Operating out of Kandahar airfield the RAF Harrier GR7 crews had arrived two years earlier – operating in support of US forces before the 3 PARA Battle Group had arrived. The Harriers provided Close Air Support (CAS) and reconnaissance for ground troops across Helmand. In addition a wide range of NATO fixed-wing aircraft were assigned to operations in Helmand. They included French and US aircraft from Kabul and Bagram who deployed to the region to ensure that Close Air Support was always available to UK forces.

Pilots formed a close bond with the ground based Joint Tactical Air Controllers (JTACs) who worked alongside the troops on the ground. The Harriers operated as pairs, with one aircraft carrying two 1,000lb Enhanced Paveway 2 laser and satellite-guided bombs, and the other armed with two rocket pods, two 500lb (227kg) dumb bombs and a reconnaissance pod. The sight of an RAF Harrier flying fast and low on a bombing mission gave great comfort to troops in contact with the enemy.

The RAF fixed-wing assets also included the Nimrod MR2, whose specialist crew was able to provide invaluable support to the Task Force. Sadly a Nimrod was lost in September 2006 when it crashed near Kandhar killing all the crew.

The repatriation ceremony at Kandahar for the Nimrod crew was very emotional for all involved.

The RAF C17 and C-130 Hercules, transport aircraft contributed heavily to the operation. The crew of a C-130 Hercules and their passengers escaped after a hard landing at Lashkar Gah which resulted in the aircraft exploding, no one was injured. The logistical challenge of delivering men and equipment to Operation HERRICK was a significant task for RAF planners. From Brize Norton the Tristar fleet airlifted the Battle Group into Kabul, then C-130 Hercules ferried troops forward to Kandahar and Bastion. With the Tristars also supporting other theatres there was little room for maintenance problems and the C-17 fleet often flew in with both passengers and urgent operational freight.

On the tarmac at Kandahar, enemy rockets flew overhead on more than one occasions as a C-17 parked up for a repatriation ceremony. Coffins were covered in the Union Jack and loaded aboard the aircraft after a church service in darkness, which added to what were already very somber occasions. Likewise it was the RAF who flew the wounded out of Helmand and into Kandahar where C-17 were transformed into flying hospitals by specialists from the RAF's aero-medical teams. These teams of doctors, nurses and specialists flew out at short notice in C-17s and provided immediate care for the wounded during the flight back to the UK.

Ground crew inspect and re-arm an RAF Harrier.

Soldiers who paid the ultimate price were flown back to the UK with full field honours.

CHAPTER TWELVE
→ **HONOURS AND AWARDS
IN MEMORIUM**

147

Captain Alex Eida, of 7 Para RHA, left, pictured during an operation. He was sadly killed on operations alongside 2nd Lieutenant Ralph Johnson of the HCR and LCpl Ross Nicholls also of the HCR. Capt Eida was later Mentioned in Dispatches in the Operational Honours and Awards list.

OPERATIONAL HONOURS AND AWARDS

AFGHANISTAN

The Victoria Cross (VC)
Corporal Bryan James BUDD
The Parachute Regiment (killed in action)

The George Cross (GC)
Corporal Mark William WRIGHT
The Parachute Regiment (killed in action)

Commander of the Order of the British Empire (CBE)
Brigadier Edward Adam BUTLER DSO MBE Late
The Royal Green Jackets

Officer of the Order of the British Empire (OBE)
Lieutenant Colonel Richard Friedrich Patrick
FELTON MBE Army Air Corps
Colonel Martin Nicholas NADIN Late
Royal Army Medical Corps

Member of the Order of the British Empire (MBE)
Lieutenant Colonel Steven Peter Walter BOYD
Corps of Royal Engineers
Major Sean Michael BURKE
The Royal Irish Regiment
Captain Marcus James DICKS
The Royal Rifle Volunteers Territorial Army
Major David James EASTMAN
Corps of Royal Electrical and Mechanical Engineers
Major Huw Spencer WILLIAMS
The Parachute Regiment

The Distinguished Service Order (DSO)
Major Paul Alan BLAIR The Parachute Regiment
Lieutenant Colonel Stuart John Craig TOOTAL OBE
The Parachute Regiment

The Conspicuous Gallantry Cross (CGC)
Lieutenant Hugo James Edward FARMER
The Parachute Regiment
Acting Captain Timothy Holden ILLINGWORTH
The Light Infantry
Lance Corporal of Horse Andrew Geoffrey RADFORD
The Life Guards

The Military Cross (MC)
Captain Douglas Ricardo BEATTIE
The Royal Irish Regiment
Second Lieutenant Oliver DALE
The Parachute Regiment
Corporal of Horse Michael John FLYNN CGC
The Blues and Royals
Staff Corporal Shaun Keith FRY
Life Guards
Corporal Stuart James GILES
The Parachute Regiment
Lance Corporal Karl Wayne JACKSON
The Parachute Regiment
Private Peter McKINLEY
The Parachute Regiment
Major Giles Matthew TIMMS
The Parachute Regiment
Captain Patrick James WILLIAMS
The Blues and Royals

Private Mark James WILSON
The Parachute Regiment
Flight Lieutenant Matthew Kenneth CARTER
Royal Air Force

The Distinguished Flying Cross (DFC)
Major Mark Christopher HAMMOND
Royal Marines
Flying Officer Christopher Michael HASLAR
Royal Air Force
Squadron Leader John Finbar MONAHAN
Royal Air Force
Flight Lieutenant Craig Thomas WILSON
Royal Air Force

The George Medal (GM)
Lance Corporal Paul HARTLEY
Royal Army Medical Corps

The Queen's Gallantry Medal (QGM)
Corporal Stuart Henry PEARSON
The Parachute Regiment

Royal Red Cross 2nd Class (ARRC)
Captain Catherine McWILLIAM
Queen Alexandra's Royal Army Nursing Corps

Mention in Despatches (MiD)
Lieutenant Nichol James Emslie BENZIE
Royal Navy
Captain Matthew Anthony William ARMSTRONG Royal
Regiment of Artillery
Private Johnnie Chad BEVANS
The Parachute Regiment
Warrant Officer Class 2 Michael John BOLTON
The Parachute Regiment
Warrant Officer Class 2 Karl Terence BRENNAN Royal
Regiment of Artillery
Captain Alexander John EIDA
Royal Regiment of Artillery (killed in action)
Captain Mark Richard EISLER
The Parachute Regiment
Corporal Stephen John FARLING
The King's Royal Hussars
Lieutenant Thomas David FEHLEY
The Parachute Regiment
Rifleman Ganesh GURUNG
The Royal Gurkha Rifles
Warrant Officer Class 2 Trilochan GURUNG
The Royal Gurkha Rifles
Corporal Benjamin Stephen HALL
Royal Army Medical Corps
Private Stephen James HALTON
The Parachute Regiment
Lieutenant Martin Joseph HEWITT
The Parachute Regiment
Lieutenant Paul Ronald HOLLINGSHEAD
The Royal Gurkha Rifles
Sergeant Daniel JARVIE
The Parachute Regiment
Warrant Officer Class 2 Thomas Heron JOHNSTONE
Army Air Corps
Corporal Kailash KHEBANG
The Royal Gurkha Rifles

Sergeant Carl Frederick LANE
The Parachute Regiment
Warrant Officer Class 2 Zachary Adam LEONG
The Parachute Regiment
Captain Alexander James MACKENZIE
The Parachute Regiment
Lance Corporal Luke Edward Patrick McCULLOCH
The Royal Irish Regiment (killed in action)
Warrant Officer Class 1 Christopher Paul MULHALL
Army Air Corps
Rifleman Nabin RAI
The Royal Gurkha Rifles
Staff Sergeant James George RANKINE
Corps of Royal Engineers
Warrant Officer Class 2 Andrew Kenneth SCHOFIELD
The Parachute Regiment
Major Toby Patrick Oughtred TILL
Coldstream Guards
Sergeant Daniel Cameron BAXTER
Royal Air Force
Sergeant Graham Martin JONES
Royal Air Force
Squadron Leader Michael John WOODS
Royal Air Force

Queen's Commendation for Bravery (QCB)
Lance Bombardier Daniel Mark BYRNE
Royal Regiment of Artillery
Warrant Officer Class 1 Andrew Steven GEE
The Royal Logistic Corps
Corporal Nicholas James GRANT
Royal Army Medical Corps
Warrant Officer Class 2 Andrew John STEDMAN
The Royal Logistic Corps

Queen's Commendation for Bravery in the Air (QCBA)
Senior Airman Jason BROLINE
United States Air Force
Staff Sergeant Cameron HYSTAD
United States Air Force

Queen's Commendation for Valuable Service (QCVS)
Colour Sergeant Stuart BELL
The Parachute Regiment
Captain Nigel John BISHOP
The Parachute Regiment
Brigadier Nicholas Roy DAVIES MBE MC Late
The Parachute Regiment
Lance Corporal Adam Spencer FEAR
Royal Corps of Signals
Lieutenant Colonel Martin Andrew FENN MBE
Corps of Royal Engineers
Colonel Charles Peter Huntley KNAGGS OBE
Late Irish Guards
Major Piers Guy Beresford STRUDWICK
The Royal Regiment of Scotland
Wing Commander Richard Francis John CLIFFORD
Royal Air Force

//CORPORAL BRYAN BUDD VC
//The Parachute Regiment

During July and August 2006, A Company, 3rd Battalion, The Parachute Regiment were deployed in the District Centre at Sangin. They were constantly under sustained attack from a combination of Taliban small arms, rocket-propelled grenades, mortar and rocket fire. On 27th July 2006 whilst on a routine patrol, Corporal Bryan Budd's section identified and engaged two enemy gunmen on the roof of a building in the centre of Sangin. During the ensuing fierce fire-fight, two of Corporal Budd's section were hit. One was seriously injured and collapsed in the open ground, where he remained exposed to enemy fire, with rounds striking the ground around him. Corporal Budd realised that he needed to regain the initiative and that the enemy needed to be driven back so that the casualty could be evacuated. Under fire, he personally led the attack on the building where the enemy fire was heaviest, driving the remaining fighters to flee across an open field where they were successfully engaged. This courageous and prompt action proved decisive in breaking the enemy and was undertaken at great personal risk. Corporal Budd's deliberate action and conspicuous gallantry allowed his wounded colleague to be evacuated to safety where he subsequently received life-saving treatment.

A month later on 20th August 2006, Corporal Budd was leading his section on the right forward flank of a platoon clearance patrol near Sangin District Centre. Another section was advancing with a Land Rover fitted with a .50 calibre heavy machine gun on the patrol's left flank. Pushing through thick vegetation, Corporal Budd identified a number of enemy fighters 30 metres ahead. Undetected and in an attempt to surprise and destroy the enemy, Corporal Budd initiated a flanking manoeuvre. However, the enemy spotted the Land Rover on the left flank and the element of surprise was lost for the whole platoon. In order to regain the initiative, Corporal Budd decided to assault the enemy and ordered his men to follow him. As they moved forward the section came under a withering fire that incapacitated three of his men. The enemy fire continued and these losses forced the section to take cover. However, Corporal Budd continued to assault forward on his own, knowing full well the likely consequences of doing so without the close support of his remaining men. He was wounded but continued to move forward, attacking and killing the enemy as he rushed their

position. Inspired by Corporal Budd's example, the rest of the platoon reorganised and pushed forward their attack, eliminating more of the enemy and eventually forcing their withdrawal. Corporal Budd subsequently died of his wounds and when his body was later recovered it was found surrounded by three dead Taliban.

Corporal Budd's conspicuous gallantry during these two engagements saved the lives of many of his colleagues. His actions were taken in the full knowledge that the rest of his men had either been struck down or had been forced to go to ground. Although wounded, his single-handed action on 20th August 2006 and his determination, though wounded, against a superior enemy force stand out as a premeditated act of inspirational leadership and the greatest valour which cost him his life. Corporal Bryan Budd's heroic actions rightly merited the award of the Victoria Cross.

//CORPORAL MARK WRIGHT GC
//The Parachute Regiment

From July 2006, a fire support group of 3rd Battalion, The Parachute Regiment, held a high ridge feature in the northern centre of Helmand Province, near the Kajaki Dam. On 6th September 2006 the leader of a sniper patrol, tasked with engaging a group of Taliban fighters operating on the principal highway, was heading down the steep slope when he initiated a mine and sustained severe injuries. Seeing the mine strike from the top of the ridge, Corporal Mark Wright gathered a number of men and rushed down the slope to assist. Realising that conducting a full mine clearance would take too long, he decided to act immediately as he knew the casualty was likely to die before the mine clearance was completed. Without thought for his own safety and fully aware of the risks he led his men into the minefield.

Corporal Wright immediately took command of the incident and directed medical orderlies to the injured soldier. Conscious of the dangers, Corporal Wright ordered all unnecessary personnel to safety and then began organising the casualty evacuation. He called for a helicopter evacuation and ordered a route to be cleared through the minefield to a landing site. Unfortunately the leader of this task also stepped on a mine when moving back across the route he believed he had cleared. Corporal Wright, again at enormous personal risk of initiating another mine, immediately moved to the new casualty and began giving life saving assistance until one of the medical orderlies could take over.

Calmly, Corporal Wright ordered all non-essential personnel to stay out of the minefield and continued to move around and control the incident. He sent accurate situation reports to his headquarters and ensured that additional medical items were obtained. Shortly afterwards a helicopter landed nearby, but as Corporal Wright stood up to get to the helicopter he initiated a third mine, sustaining serious injuries to himself and one of the orderlies. The remaining medical orderly began treating Corporal Wright, but was himself wounded by another mine blast which caused further injury to both Corporal Wright and others. There were now seven casualties still in the minefield. Despite this horrific situation and the serious injuries to himself and others, Corporal Wright continued to command and control the incident. He remained conscious for the majority of the time, continually shouting encouragement to those around him. This maintained morale and calm amongst the many wounded men. Sadly, Corporal Wright died of his wounds in the rescue helicopter.

His outstandingly courageous actions and leadership were an inspiration to his men. For acts of the greatest gallantry and complete disregard for his own safety in striving to save others, he was awarded the George Cross.

//ACTING CAPTAIN TIMOTHY ILLINGWORTH CGC
//Light Infantry

On 10th September 2006, Lieutenant Timothy Illingworth deployed with a small team in support of a joint Afghan Police and Army operation to recapture Garmser District Centre. During two days of heavy fighting, Lieutenant Illingworth and his team were constantly under fire whilst motivating, directing and advising their Afghan colleagues who successfully re-took Garmser. Later that week an Afghan Police patrol supported by Lieutenant Illingworth's team was ambushed resulting in one British casualty. In an effort to relieve the pressure on the Afghan Police, he led his Afghan company commander and a foot patrol to neutralise the enemy position. This inspired his Afghan Army colleagues who were reticent to advance on the heavily defended enemy position.

The Afghani resolve to continue failed after three days of heavy fighting. Seeing this, Lieutenant Illingworth went to the front of the Afghan troops and moved alone to within 30 metres of the first enemy position under heavy fire. Soon after, the Afghan Company Commander was killed. Lieutenant Illingworth took up the commander's rocket launcher, firing three rounds into the main enemy position in full view of them. He himself narrowly missed being killed. All but one of the Afghan force abandoned Lieutenant Illingworth, leaving him exposed and under withering fire. In spite of his isolation, he attempted to assault the enemy position expending seven magazines of ammunition. The enemy fire was unrelenting. He regrouped and rallied the remaining force to continue. Lieutenant Illingworth's bravery and example over seven days were well beyond the call of duty. His role was to mentor rather than fight. However, understanding the importance of Garmser, he placed himself in a position of utmost danger to influence events. His outstanding courage, leadership and selflessness in pressing home his attack upset the enemy ambush and saved many lives. Such inspiring and raw courage from a relatively young and inexperienced officer was exemplary and justly merited the award of the Conspicuous Gallantry Cross.

//FLIGHT LIEUTENANT MATTHEW CARTER MC
//Royal Air Force Regiment

On 4th June 2006, Flight Lieutenant Matthew Carter of the Royal Air Force Regiment was deployed with 16 Air Assault Brigade on an operation against a suspected Taliban compound outside the town of Now Zad in Helmand Province. During the first of three contacts, he coordinated and directed close and accurate Attack Helicopter fire support with devastating results for Taliban ground troops. During the last contact, he left his vehicle fearlessly exposing himself to significant risk as he forced his way to the front of the firefight to join the forward troops. This enabled him to direct aerial cannon fire against a determined enemy 30 metres in front of him. This risk was essential given the ferocious weight of the incoming fire from the Taliban.

His direction of these engagements proved critical, destroying the enemy location completely on one occasion. He remained with the lead dismounted elements of Patrols Platoon and took part in the immediate compound clearance.

During this time Carter repeatedly exposed himself to a significant chance of being killed and, because of this gallant behaviour in supporting his unit he enabled the Patrols Platoon to regain the initiative.

On 14th July Carter participated in a Battle Group operation to capture or kill a high value Taliban leader. During the insertion to the helicopter landing site the first wave of Chinook helicopters were heavily engaged by Taliban machine gun and RPG fire causing the aircraft to lift off again, after only 20 seconds on the ground. Fearing being left behind on the aircraft, Carter jumped some 15 feet from the tail ramp into the darkness, realising the vital role he had to play in calling in air support to suppress the enemy. Immediately he got into the cover of a nearby ditch and called in an aircraft to destroy the principal threat of an enemy machine gun. He controlled the aircraft's heavy attacks, which were close to his own location and destroyed the Taliban position only a few metres away. This significant and gallant contribution by Flight Lieutenant Carter proved to be decisive in allowing the remaining aircraft to land the rest of the Battle Group to complete the mission successfully. For this act of selfless bravery he was awarded the Military Cross.

//LIEUTENANT HUGO FARMER CGC
//The Parachute Regiment

Throughout 3 PARA's tour of Afghanistan, Lieutenant Hugo Farmer commanded 1 Platoon A Company in some of the most intensive engagements of the tour. During this time he consistently demonstrated outstanding leadership and gallantry. On 27th July 2006, when defending the District Centre in Sangin against determined attack by the Taliban, his platoon was engaged by gunmen and two of his men were wounded. On 30th July 2006, his platoon was attacked once again and Lieutenant Farmer personally led an assault onto the enemy in the building. His prompt action regained the initiative and forced the Taliban to flee.

On a clearance patrol on 17th August 2006, Lieutenant Farmer identified and engaged enemy fighters resulting in a vicious firefight. Under effective hostile fire, he organised supporting artillery fire and then personally led an assault on the enemy positions killing a number and forcing them to withdraw. Lieutenant Farmer organised a snap ambush and inflicted significant enemy casualties, thereby allowing his platoon to proceed unharmed.

On 20th August 2006, Lieutenant Farmer's lead Section became engaged in a heavy firefight and soon had three soldiers incapacitated, forcing a withdrawal. This situation was further complicated by the fact that Corporal Budd, the lead section commander, was reported as missing having

continued to assault the enemy position on his own. Lieutenant Farmer quickly reorganised his Platoon and led two attempts with his remaining Sections in an attempt to locate Corporal Budd.

Driven back by increasingly heavy fire, he was forced to adopt a defensive position until reinforcements arrived. Lieutenant Farmer continued to consolidate his position, fighting off repeated Taliban attacks. On the arrival of Apache helicopters, he directed their fire to suppress the enemy before personally leading one Section to find and evacuate his injured section commander. Lieutenant Farmer displayed considerable courage and personal example under fire, inspiring his men in a dangerous and confusing situation where casualties had been sustained.

Lieutenant Farmer's actions over a three month period were undertaken in the full knowledge of the significant risks he faced. Often under intense fire, he never hesitated to lead from the front. His courage and inspirational leadership contributed significantly to decisive defeats inflicted on the enemy and merited the award of the Conspicuous Gallantry Cross.

//LANCE CORPORAL OF HORSE ANDREW RADFORD CGC
//Household Cavalry Regiment

On 1st August 2006, Lance Corporal of Horse Andrew Radford's Troop of the Household Cavalry Regiment was deployed in Southern Afghanistan. As his Troop moved through a small village, the lead two vehicles were ambushed by Taliban forces with a combination of Rocket Propelled Grenade fire, heavy machine guns and a large Improvised Explosive Device. One of the vehicles was badly damaged in the initial attack, killing three of its four occupants immediately. The driver of the vehicle was badly injured but still alive whilst the vehicle continued to burn fiercely. The crew of the second vehicle managed to extract themselves from the ambush whilst under accurate enemy rocket fire, but had to abandon their vehicle in the process.

Seeing the imminent danger that the driver of the abandoned vehicle was in, and without hesitation or prompting from his officer, Lance Corporal of Horse Radford dismounted from his vehicle under sustained enemy fire and ran into the ambush killing area towards the gravely injured driver.

Entering into a scene of utter devastation and horror, Radford reached his injured comrade.

He showed an almost superhuman effort in carrying the wounded trooper back 70 metres uphill to his own armoured vehicle under challenging conditions. This feat was all the more remarkable as at the time he was still under heavy fire from a mixture of machine guns and Rocket Propelled Grenades. Lance Corporal of Horse Radford showed a complete disregard for his own safety and acted completely on his own initiative. A father of four young children, he deliberately put himself in harm's way and was utterly focussed on saving his comrade in trouble, who had suffered horrendous injuries. Without doubt, his immediate action saved his colleague's life and justified the award of the Conspicuous Gallantry Cross.

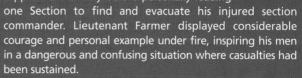

//MAJOR MARK HAMMOND DFC

//Royal Marines

On the night of 6th September 2006, Major Mark Hammond, Royal Marines, was a pilot deployed to Afghanistan with No. 18(B) Squadron. His Chinook crew were on standby when the Sangin platoon house was attacked, resulting in one soldier suffering a life-threatening injury. Despite the known threat of Taliban anti-aircraft weapons, his aircraft was scrambled to retrieve the casualty accompanied by two Apache Helicopters. As the overall Mission Leader, Major Hammond directed the Apaches to remain overhead while he made a quick and aggressive approach in order to land. On departing the landing site with the casualty, the aircraft was engaged by ground machine gun fire. Using outstanding piloting skills, Major Hammond successfully carried out evasive manoeuvres while the crewmen returned fire and the aircraft escaped unscathed.

On arrival at Camp Bastion, he was immediately directed to return to Musa Qala to recover another critical casualty.

The only available landing site however was next to the compound that had just been attacked. Despite the serious risk to his aircraft and crew, Major Hammond began a fast and low approach, but the weight of accurate ground fire forced the landing to be aborted. The supporting Apaches witnessed two rocket propelled grenades pass just 10 meters above and below the Chinook and all three crewmen returned fire in an attempt to suppress the firing points, killing at least two Taliban.

On returning to base, four rounds were found to have hit Hammond's aircraft, one causing serious and almost catastrophic damage to a blade root. At this stage it would have been simple for Major Hammond to declare that thethreat was too high to return to Musa Qala. But without hesitation he decided to attempt another recovery using a new aircraft. The mission was an outstanding success under heavy fire. Any one of the three separate engagements on the night of 6th September would have been sufficient to shake most men, but Major Hammond remained calm, resolute and dedicated throughout and his actions merited the award of the Distinguished Flying Cross.

A Chinook firing its chaff flare system to deflect a potential missile attack.

154

The memorial cairn at camp Bastion.

IN MEMORIAM

Two soldiers died during preliminary operations: Corporal Mark Cridge of 7 Signals Regiment and LCpl Peter Edward Craddock of 1st Battalion The Royal Gloucestershire, Berkshire and Wiltshire Regiment. Both were non-combat deaths.

Captain Jim Philippson of 7th Parachute Regiment Royal Horse Artillery died on 11 June 2006 while on operations in Helmand Province. He was killed in an incident on the evening of Sunday 11 June 2006 during which a mobile patrol was engaged in a firefight against suspected Taliban forces. Sadly as a result of this engagement Captain Jim Philippson was killed and two other soldiers seriously injured.

Captain David Patten of The Parachute Regiment died on 27 June 2006 during operations in Helmand Province. Capt Patten who was serving on special duties in support of the 3 PARA BG was killed during a planned operation in the Sangin valley, northern Helmand province, in the early morning of 27 June, his patrol came under attack and Capt Patten was killed.

Sgt Paul BartleTt of the Royal Marines died on 27 June 2006 during operations in Helmand Province. Sgt Bartlett who was serving on special duties in support of the 3 PARA BG was killed during a planned operation in the Sangin valley, northern Helmand province, in the early morning of 27 June, the patrol came under attack and Sgt Bartlett was killed.

Cpl Peter Thorpe of 216 Parachute Squadron Royal Signals, died on operations in Helmand Province on 1st July 2006. He was killed when a Taliban rocket hit a building at Sangin as he carried out a key role in support of 3 PARA. Corporal Thorpe joined the Army in August 1995 as an apprentice tradesman at Harrogate and went on to complete his communications training at the Royal School of Signals at Blandford, Dorset.

LCpl Jabron Hashmi of the Intelligence Corps, died on operations in Helmand Province on 1st July 2006. He was killed when a Taliban rocket hit a building at Sangin, where attached to 216 Signals Squadron, he was carrying out a key role in support of 3 PARA. Lance Corporal Hashmi joined the Army in June 2004 and completed his trade training at the Army Training Centre Winchester and his intelligence training at Chicksands, Bedfordshire.

Private Damien Jackson of The Parachute Regiment died on operations in Helmand Province on the 6th July 2006. He was killed during operations against the Taliban in the Sangin valley while serving with A Company of the 3rd Battalion The Parachute Regiment. He joined the Regiment in 2004, Damien quickly made his mark within the Battalion and served in numerous theatres including Northern Ireland and Iraq.

Captain Alex Eida of 7 Parachute Regiment Royal Horse Artillery, died on operations in Helmand on the 1st August 2006. He was killed while serving as a Forward Observation Officer during an engagement with the Taliban. He first saw military service with the TA while studying for his degree at the University of Glamorgan. He then worked as an instructor with Camp USA and as a ski rep before attending the RMA Sandhurst and being commissioned into the Royal Artillery.

2nd Lieutenant Ralph Johnson of the Household Cavalry Regiment, died on 1st August 2006 during operations against the Taliban in Helmand Province. He was working with Capt Alex Eida and LCpl Ross Nicholls when he was killed. He had joined the Life Guards in August 2005

LCpl Ross Nicholls of the Household Cavalry Regiment died on operations against the Taliban on 1st August 2006. He was working with Capt Alex Eida and 2nd Lieutenant Ralph Johnson when he was killed. LCpl Nicholls had joined the Royal Signals in August 1995 before transferring to the Blues and Royals in July 2004.

Private Andrew Barrie Cutts of 13 Regiment Royal Logistic Corps died on the 6th August 2006 during Operation Snakebite at Musa Qaleh in Helmand. He joined the Army in July 2003. Following basic training he was posted as a driver into 13 Air Assault Support Regiment, The Royal Logistic Corps, based in Colchester. Private Cutts deployed to Afghanistan on 11 March 2006 as part of the Regiment's Force Protection Troop.

LCpl Sean Tansey of the Household Cavalry died on 12th August 2006 while on operational deployment in Helmand. He was killed in a tragic accident involving a British military vehicle undergoing routine maintenance. Lance Corporal Sean Tansey, from Washington, Tyne and Wear, enlisted into The Life Guards in May 1999. In 2003 he deployed with D Squadron to Iraq, where the Squadron and his troop were in numerous contacts with Iraqi forces, ahead of 16 Air Assault Brigade.

Cpl Bryan James Budd VC of The Parachute Regiment died during offensive operations against the Taliban on 20th August 2006. Cpl Budd died in a fierce firefight with enemy forces at Sangin. He had joined the Army in 1995 and enjoyed a distinguished career with service with the Pathfinders before joining A Company, 3 PARA, in early June 2006.

LCpl Jonathan Peter Hetherington of 14 Signal Regiment (Electronic Warfare), died on 27th August following an attack on the Platoon House in Musa Qaleh, northern Helmand Province. He had earlier deployed on Op TELIC 1, serving in Kuwait and Iraq, and also the Falkland Islands. He joined the Army in September 2000 and initially served with 249 Signal Squadron after training.

Ranger Anare Draiva of the 1st Battalion The Royal Irish Regiment died on 1st September during an incident in Helmand province at 1600 local time. The 27 year-old Fijian soldier was highly respected and liked across his battalion. During the Taliban attack a colleague (LCpl Muirhead) was seriously injured, and died later.

Cpl Oliver Simon Dicketts of 1st Battalion,The Parachute Regiment was assigned to specialist duties with the RAF when he died on 2nd Setpember in the RAF Nimrod MR2 crash near Kandahar. He had joined The Parachute Regiment in 2000 and after completing his training in 2001 was posted to 1st Battalion The Parachute Regiment in Dover.

LCpl Paul Muirhead of the 1st Battalion The Royal Irish Regiment died on Wednesday 6th September as a result of wounds sustained during a Taliban attack on his base at Musa Quala in Helmand Province on Friday 1st September 2006. Since the attack, he had been receiving specialist medical care and his parents were with him when he died.

Cpl Mark William Wright GC of 3rd Battalion The Parachute Regiment died in Helmand Province on 6th September when his patrol encountered an unmarked minefield near Kajaki. Cpl Wright joined the Army in January 1999 was posted to the 3rd Battalion, The Parachute Regiment later that year. He had completed three tours of Northern Ireland and in 2003, he deployed, along with the 3rd Battalion, to Iraq where he served with distinction.

LCpl Luke McCulloch of the 1st Battalion The Royal Irish Regiment died in Helmand on 6th September following a contact with Taliban forces in Sangin, Helmand province. Luke joined the Army in 2001. After completing his basic training he joined a Rifle Company and after a short period joined the Reconnaissance Platoon. He was an enthusiastic soldier, held in high regard by all ranks in the Battalion, who served with distinction on tours of Northern Ireland, Iraq and Afghanistan.

THE RAF NIMROD MR2 CREW LOST OVER KANDAHAR, SERVING IN SUPPORT OF THE UKTF.

Flt Lt Steven Johnson
Flt Lt Leigh Anthony Mitchelmore
Flt Lt Gareth Rodney Nicholas
Flt Lt Allan James Squires
Flt Lt Steven Swarbrick
FS Gary Wayne Andrews
FS Stephen Beattie
FS Gerard Martin Bell
FS Adrian Davies
Sgt Benjamin James Knight
Sgt John Joseph Langton
Sgt Gary Paul Quilliam
Cpl Oliver Simon Dicketts, The Parachute Regiment
Marine Joseph David Windall Royal Marines Poole